Technology for Small and One-Person Libraries

Technology for Small and One-Person Libraries

A LITA Guide

Rene J. Erlandson
and
Rachel A. Erb

ALA TechSource
An imprint of the American Library Association

CHICAGO   2013

Printed in the United States of America

17 16 15 14 13   5 4 3 2 1

Extensive effort has gone into ensuring the reliability of the information in this book; however, the publisher makes no warranty, express or implied, with respect to the material contained herein.

ISBNs: 978-1-55570-858-0 (paper); 978-1-55570-871-9 (PDF); 978-1-55570-872-6 (ePub); 978-1-55570-873-3 (Kindle).

Library of Congress Cataloging-in-Publication Data

Erlandson, Rene J., author.
    Technology for Small and One-Person Libraries : A LITA guide / Rene J. Erlandson, Rachel A. Erb.
        pages cm. -— (A LITA Guide)
    Includes bibliographical references and index.
    ISBN 978-1-55570-858-0
    1. Small libraries—Data processing—Handbooks, manuals, etc. 2. Library science—Data processing-—Handbooks, manuals, etc. 3. Small libraries—Automation—Planning—Handbooks, manuals, etc. 4. Small libraries—Information technology—Planning. 5. Libraries—Automation—Planning. 6. Libraries—Information technology—Planning. 7. Library information networks. I. Erb, Rachel A., author. II. Title.
    Z678.93.S6E75 2013
    025.00285—dc23   2012040945

Book design in Berkeley and Avenir. Cover image © Adchariyaphoto/Shutterstock, Inc.

♾ This paper meets the requirements of ANSI/NISO Z39.48-1992 (Permanence of Paper).

Contents

Contents

Preface

Technology for Small and One-Person Libraries: A LITA Guide is designed to help librarians working in institutions with little technical support to successfully develop, implement, sustain, and grow technology initiatives. Technology is often viewed by librarians as a living entity, simultaneously revered and hated, something librarians must control or libraries will go the way of the dinosaur—dying, becoming extinct and thus irrelevant. The truth is less dramatic. Technology is a means to an end. Technology provides the infrastructure and tools librarians can use to serve their communities.

The persistent focus on technology in library literature in recent years might lead one to believe technology has only influenced libraries in the past few decades. However, technology has impacted libraries since the inception of the institution. The earliest known library at Nineveh consisted of information recorded on clay tablets, the Library at Alexandria provided researchers access to knowledge housed on scrolls, and the Roman codex quickly found its way into libraries, as a more portable form for information. Fast-forward to microfiche, microfilm, LPs, videotapes, floppy discs, CDs, DVDs, flash drives, direct access computer services, remote access computer services, streaming movies/music, e-books, and all the accompanying equipment needed to access information stored in these various media, and the impact of technology on libraries is clearly more far-reaching than just the past thirty years.

Most of us who chose librarianship as a career did not come to it because we wanted to be information technology professionals. However, to examine the history of libraries is to see a record of technological advancements. From the codex to the World Wide Web, technology has continually pushed librarians to redefine the institution, and thus the profession, within the culture. As technology evolves, librarians adopt and adapt newly developed tools to serve their communities.

Today, many librarians actively cull the technological landscape to discover new ways to connect and communicate with their communities.

ORGANIZATION AND CONTENT

This technology guide is for librarians, library staff, and administrators working at small and one-person libraries serving populations of 15,000 or less, who have little experience managing or implementing technology but have a desire to do so. The guide provides basic, practical information on a variety of technology-related topics and will be useful to those working in libraries with limited resources.

The book is divided into three sections: Library Technology Basics, e-Resources, and The Virtual Library. Each section contains multiple chapters that explain fundamental concepts, introduce different aspects of technology, and include practical advice and best practices for implementing specific technologies. Useful books, articles, and websites pertaining to the technology covered within each chapter are noted as sources of additional information throughout the book.

Library Technology Basics provides a framework for understanding technology in libraries. In chapter 1, Rene Erlandson equips readers with a step-by-step guide for developing a library technology plan to facilitate future strategic technology decisions. Chapter 2 highlights hardware and software commonly used in libraries, including workstations and mobile devices like laptops, netbooks, tablets, and e-Readers. In chapter 3, Scott Childers outlines the fundamental principles of infrastructure/networking in libraries, including an overview of cloud computing. He also provides practical advice for setting up librarywide networks—like LAN and Wi-Fi. Rachel Erb introduces integrated library systems (ILS) in chapter 4 and compares and contrasts the features of specific low-cost and open-source ILS options.

In chapter 5, Rachel Erb outlines fundamental concepts of e-resources and examines options for managing and integrating e-resources into library collections. Chapter 6 outlines electronic resource license agreement structure and language, highlighting issues to be aware of regarding use and lending when negotiating e-resource license agreements with vendors.

Chapters 7–11 in The Virtual Library emphasize integrating existing and emerging technologies in libraries. Chapter 7 explains website development for both desktop and mobile users, including best practices and low-cost and open-source platform options and development tools. Chapter 8 outlines how libraries can capitalize on popular social media platforms to serve community members and promote the library. Chapter 9 highlights specific open-source library applications available to libraries and examines their uses. In chapter 10, Nicci Westbrook outlines strategies for creating digital collections and explores available free collection mounting and hosting options. In chapter 11, Rene Erlandson wraps up by spotlighting ways to find technology assistance outside your organization and keep up with future technology trends in libraries.

—Rene J. Erlandson

Acknowledgments

Thank you to LITA, Neal-Schuman, and ALA for the opportunity to work on this project, specifically Charles Harmon, Marta Deyrup, Patrick Hogan, Alison Elms, and Patricia Stahl. I also wish to formally acknowledge the contributions of Scott Childers and Nicci Westbrook; I enjoyed serving as the editor for the chapters they wrote as well as those written by Rachel Erb, who began working on this project as systems librarian at the University of Nebraska Omaha. In addition, a special thanks to Dr. Thomas J. McDonnell for his assistance throughout this project. I am fortunate to have worked with an array of fantastic individuals throughout my career, and although space constraints prohibit me from mentioning each individually, I am grateful to all. I would specifically like to acknowledge the mentorship and guidance of Sharon E. Clark, Barton Clark, John M. Littlewood, and Karen Lawson and the unflagging support of Sharon Murray, Virginia Clark, Linda Mowry, and Glenda J. Wilson. I would also be remiss if I did not thank Marilyn and Ruby for teaching me the value of education, hard work, and determination; Jerry for his support; and Tom and Maisie—for every minute of every day.

—*R. J. Erlandson*

I want to thank the LITA Publications Committee for supporting this publication and allowing us the opportunity to reach librarians working in small and one-person libraries. I sincerely appreciate our editor Marta Deyrup's quick and helpful editorial suggestions. Finally, I am forever indebted to my husband, Brian, for his patience, feedback, and encouragement during the past several months, and for my fellow first-generation college students and graduates everywhere.

—*Rachel A. Erb*

PART 1

Library Technology Basics

Technology Plan Fundamentals

Rene J. Erlandson

In its early days, librarians often likened the Internet to the interstate highway system. One accessed the Internet at various points along an established route, exited at a desired location, and then entered back onto the highway to travel to the next location. The transportation metaphor also works to describe a technology plan. A technology plan is a road map of a journey; it shows where you began, where you currently are, and where you ultimately want to go. There are many factors to consider when planning a journey, and many issues can influence the routes chosen to reach desired destinations on the map.

A technology plan generally consists of six elements:

- Introduction
- Technology vision statement
- Overview of past technology initiatives
- Synopsis of the current technology environment
- Future technology goals and objectives, timeline and assessment methods
- Budget

This chapter will explain how to develop a flexible and sustainable framework for incorporating technology into the library. By following the steps outlined here and using tools mentioned throughout the chapter, you will be able to develop a successful plan.

WHY CREATE A LIBRARY TECHNOLOGY PLAN?

As new technologies emerge with increasing frequency, libraries struggle to determine which high-tech developments to implement and how to incorporate them into their daily routines and services. Some libraries hop on every trend that comes along, before considering if the new technology meets a need or not, or how to sustain the program once it is implemented. Other libraries jump from one initiative to another, without ever fully developing or assessing the impact of any single implementation. This disorganized approach is inefficient at best. At worst, the inadequate preparation, implementation, and assessment of initiatives may result in abandoned or static programs. A technology plan examines the history of the library's previous technology initiatives, identifies current technology programs, sets future technology goals and objectives, and lays a course for assessment and review. By developing a technology plan and using it to inform technology decisions, libraries can ensure that future initiatives will support their mission in the community and avoid costly mistakes.

External forces may also dictate the need to craft a technology plan. Libraries affiliated with city or state governments or with other institutions that require formal documents, such as strategic plans, may be required to submit a technology plan. Although libraries seeking Federal Communications Commission (FCC) e-rate discounts on Internet-related infrastructure costs such as telecommunications charges and network-related expenses are no longer required to submit a technology plan as part of the application process to the University Service Administrative Company, some agencies still require e-rate applicants to have a technology plan on file with the certifying agency prior to certification of any applications. In addition, some corporate, foundation, and federal grant applications require evidence of local technology planning.

Regardless of whether the impetus is internal or external, a technology plan should be an evolving document used and understood by all levels of library staff. A technology plan should not be developed, formalized, and then put in a drawer to be brought out only when or if a governing agency requires it. Development of a technology plan is only a useful exercise if there is a commitment to continued use of the framework as a means of directing the deployment of technology within an institution over time.

STEPS TO DEVELOPING A LIBRARY TECHNOLOGY PLAN

Gather the Team

When developing a technology plan, try to recruit people with diverse perspectives. While one individual can create a library technology plan, forming a team will increase the knowledge base and the skill sets from which the plan will be drawn. Team size will vary depending on circumstances. Identify individuals associated with the library who are affected by library technology initiatives. Some obvious technology stakeholder groups are library staff, library patrons, friends of the library, library administrators, and technology support staff outside of the library, such as campus or city information technology professionals. By tapping these individuals, librarians working in small or one-person libraries can gain valuable expertise and insight.

Compile the Introduction Statement

Begin the technology plan with a statement that provides general information about the library, the team that is developing the plan, the process for developing the plan, and the timeline for review and revision of the plan. Also include the library mission statement within the introduction. The library mission statement can generally be found at the beginning of the library's strategic plan. This section need only be a paragraph or two, but it can be expanded if desired.

Craft Library Technology Vision Statement

Like the introduction, the library technology vision statement does not need to be lengthy or complicated. At its core, the statement explains how technology will be used to support the mission of the library. This statement is an important first

Urbana Free Public Library Vision Statement

"In keeping with [its] mission, The Urbana Free Library is committed to the use of technology to improve the quality, scope, and efficiency of library services. The library continually reviews and adopts new technology to enhance the library experience of its users, to help library users achieve their goals, to improve access to information, and to improve employees' ability to perform their duties."

step in charting future technology initiatives because it should inform all future technology-related decisions. When technology is viewed as a tool to facilitate achievement of the institution's objectives and goals, it is understood to be a means to an end and not an end in itself. This is important because most successful technology initiatives serve a purpose—they solve a problem or support a need.

Begin to craft the vision statement by reading the library's mission statement. Consider how technology can be used to support the library mission and to accomplish its stated goals. Remember, the vision statement should be overarching and concise (see sidebar). The vision statement will not reference specific initiatives; those will be outlined later in the technology plan.

Identify Past Library Technology Initiatives

Once a library technology vision statement is crafted, begin mapping the library's technology plan by looking at past initiatives. Did the library bring up an online public access catalog (OPAC), a next generation catalog, or a mobile catalog? Does the library have a website? Is reference service provided via telephone, e-mail, instant messaging, or text messaging? Are desktop computers available in the library for public use? Does the library circulate laptops, netbooks, e-book readers? Is there free Wi-Fi in the building? Although initiatives such as an online public access catalog, telephone reference service, and website may have been implemented many years ago, at the time they were implemented, each was an emerging technology initiative.

After compiling the list of past technology initiatives, rate the success level of each. Consider the reasons for ranking each initiative as you did. Is the OPAC successful because people stopped asking for the card catalog or because visitors link directly to full-text books or articles? Is the website successful because community members have commented on its attractiveness or because it receives a lot of hits every month? Is the public computer workstation initiative successful because of the number of people who use workstations per week, or because they draw in a segment of the population that previously did not use the library? Identifying characteristics of successful past projects provides a basis for determining benchmarks to be used to rate the success of future initiatives. A sample worksheet that can be used to track past initiatives is shown in table 1.1.

As the team discusses past initiatives, consider them in relation to the vision statement just crafted. Which programs supported the library mission? Which programs solved a specific problem or met a need? Were any programs implemented

TABLE 1.1
Past Technology Initiatives Worksheet

Initiative	Success level (5 being the most successful)	Reasons for level of success
	5 4 3 2 1	
	5 4 3 2 1	
	5 4 3 2 1	
	5 4 3 2 1	
	5 4 3 2 1	
	5 4 3 2 1	
	5 4 3 2 1	

that did not serve a direct purpose, and if so, how successful were they? If the newly crafted vision statement had existed, would each initiative have been implemented? Identify the most successful and the least successful elements of past initiatives and refer to these characteristics when considering future initiatives.

Use information gleaned through team discussions and from the compiled list to draft a short history of technology in the library, being sure to note significant successful initiatives. The length of this section will vary from a paragraph to multiple pages depending on the number of initiatives implemented locally and how much detail is desired.

Inventory Current Technology Environment

Performing an inventory of the existing library technology environment clarifies how technology is currently integrated into library services and pinpoints exactly where current resources are deployed. Your inventory should include hardware and software; infrastructure networks; servers; Wi-Fi; cloud computing; integrated library system (ILS); digital collections; institutional repository or other online archive and web services, including library web pages, social media and social networking pages, mobile web pages, or mobile apps. Compile a list of every technology-related program and service the library offers.

Just as in the previous step, consider each initiative in relation to the recently crafted technology vision statement. If the statement had been in place at the time the decision was being made to implement the technology, would the initiative have been approved? Identify how each initiative supports the library's mission and align each initiative with a specific objective. How successful is each current initiative? Are there opportunities for growth? What characteristics do past and present successful initiatives share? Refer to these insights later when drafting future objectives and goals. Consider eliminating initiatives that do not support the mission of the library, do not fill an identifiable need, or are ranked unsuccessful.

Once the list of current initiatives is compiled, identify who is responsible for maintaining each program on the list. Accounting for the vagaries of organizational life such as staff turnover or a departmental reorganization, it is critical that current programs are carefully tracked so they will not be abandoned. Maintenance is crucial to the success of any technology initiative. Therefore, when developing a technology plan, it is important to know what the current initiatives are and who is responsible for maintaining them. A sample worksheet for depicting a library's current technology environment is shown in table 1.2.

At this point, it is also useful to assess the technology skills and interests of current staff. Library jobs often require specific skill sets, so many managers inquire only about requisite proficiencies when interviewing potential employees. In addition, many candidates fail to mention technology skills developed while working on personal projects because they have no formal training. However, skills developed when creating the website for a family reunion or authoring a blog for the local running club can easily be applied to maintaining the library's website or contributing to its social networking pages. Also, consider whether training staff to obtain a specific skill set or augmenting existing skills through professional development could improve the success level of existing technology initiatives. Online webinars or noncredit courses at a local community college in blogging, web design, or social media marketing strategies might be affordable, accessible options for training staff. Good managers capitalize on as many skills and interests of employees as possible, increasing library resources and empowering library staff. Once an assessment of staff technology expertise is completed, include a general note on the overall level of staff expertise in the inventory of the current technology environment.

Future Technology Goals and Objectives

Many libraries begin the planning process by thinking about the future, which is much like leaving on a trip without a map or GPS, having no idea what the final destination is like, taking along only the money in your pocket, not knowing which

TABLE 1.2
Current Library Technology Environment Worksheet

Initiative/project/service	Who maintains the initiative/ project/service
Public/Staff Workstations	
Software	
Cloud computing service	
Network infrastructure	
Servers	
In-building Wi-Fi	
Circulating equipment: • Laptop/netbook • eBook reader (Kindle, Nook, etc.) • iPad • Digital camera • Digital video camera	
ILS	
Website	
Mobile Website/Apps	
Library related blogs (list all)	
LibGuides	
YouTube Channel	
Flickr collection	
Facebook page(s)	
Twitter page/account	
Institutional repository or other online archive	
Digital collections (list all)	
Email/IM/SMS Reference	
Other:	
Other:	
Other:	

language is commonly used, what there is to do locally, or if you can afford the food and hotel. Although spontaneity is liberating, its outcomes are unpredictable. Most libraries do not have unlimited resources to throw at every new trend that comes along and therefore need to maximize the impact of their technology investments through planning.

The goals and objectives defined within this portion of the plan as well as the timeline outlined here will be the framework for future initiatives. This section of the document will include all technology initiatives that will be supported during the lifetime of the document. So, if the document covers the next three years, include existing technology initiatives that will be maintained during the time period as well as new initiatives that will be implemented. Example: the library plans to continue to maintain the existing library website. Goal: maintain existing library website. Objective: Sheila will review the content of the library website at least once a month. Refer back to the inventory of the current technology environment from the last step and carefully examine whether each initiative will be maintained in the future. Eliminate programs that do not support the mission of the library or do not fill a need.

Once continuing initiatives are accounted for, identify technology needs that are not being met. Relate potential initiatives to library service priorities. For example, the library's advertising budget has been reduced and a daily ad in the local newspaper is no longer possible, but you still want to let people know about events, programs, and services. Reaching out to community members through popular online social networking platforms may be a way to promote the library. Goal: promote the library via social networking sites. Objective 1: create a Facebook Fan page. Objective 2: create a Twitter stream.

Determine if existing library technology can be used to accomplish goals and objectives, or if hardware and software need to be upgraded or purchased. Continuing the earlier example; Facebook and Twitter accounts are free and require only a computer connected to the Internet, a browser, and an account on the specified platform; therefore, the goal and associated objectives can be accomplished with existing resources.

Next, identify staff to implement and maintain an initiative. Will training be needed for those directly responsible for the project? Will job descriptions need to be adjusted? Is training of other staff necessary? If the answer to any of these questions is yes, add objectives to the corresponding goal. Example: update Sheila's job description to include responsibility for creating and maintaining the Facebook Fan page and Twitter stream.

Also, consider if a project impacts any existing library policies. Will the initiative necessitate new policies? Example: libraries venturing into social media or social networking for the first time will want to establish a policy to govern interactions within library-sponsored sites. Objective: develop a library social media and social network policy. (For more information on developing a library social media and social networking policy see chapter 8 of this book.)

Next, establish a timeline for implementing, maintaining, and assessing each initiative. Include details such as how often an initiative needs to be updated and who will be responsible for the updates. Example: the library Facebook status will be updated at least three times a week and the library Twitter stream will be updated once a day by Sheila.

Assessment is the portion of technology planning that is often overlooked. Once a project is realized, thinking that it is complete is a fallacy. Unless a project is maintained it is unlikely to flourish, and without assessment further allocation of resources to a project will be difficult to justify. The more successful a project, the higher priority it should be given for future funding. But how do you determine if a project is successful? Look back at the list of past technology projects compiled earlier in this process. What criteria were used to rate the success of each? There are no rules or standards for measuring success, so brainstorm with team members to come up with possible measures. Assessment criteria should be measurable and reasonable, so define realistic benchmarks for each initiative to determine its success and develop a timeline for assessment. Example: the library is experimenting with social media. Objective one: develop 100 Facebook Fan or Friend connections in the first year the library fan page exists. Objective two: obtain one hundred followers of the library's Twitter stream in the first year.

Develop a Budget for Each Initiative

Some initiatives, like creating a Facebook Fan page may be accomplished with existing resources; however, others, like providing free Wi-Fi, migrating to a virtual machine environment, launching cloud computing, or moving to a new integrated library system, may require substantial investment. Administrators and governing boards will want to know the costs associated with each initiative and where the money will come from.

When developing a technology plan budget, also be sure to mention external funding options and note them in the budget and in the goals and objectives portion of the document. Applying for a grant, soliciting donations, or applying for

9

discounted services are steps that need to be included when creating the timeline for implementation. Writing a grant proposal, contacting prospective donors, and creating necessary documentation for potential funding should be reflected in the objectives of the related goal. If a project necessitates bids from vendors, suppliers, or contractors, a request for a proposal may be necessary and should also be included in the timeline and objectives.

Review and Update Plan

A technology plan guides technology decisions. Therefore, in order to remain relevant over time the plan must be reviewed and updated regularly. Individuals responsible for implementing and maintaining technology initiatives outlined in the plan should refer to it often and note changes as needed. For example, if the timeline for developing a Facebook fan page was three months, but the person who was supposed to implement the project had to take a two month leave of absence, either the project will need to be reassigned or the timeline will need to be adjusted. The plan will need to be updated to reflect the change.

Generally technology plans are created for specific time periods dictated by a governing institution or grant requirement. Begin the process of crafting a new technology plan approximately six months to a year before the designated end of the current technology plan. Members of the former planning team will be familiar

Examples of Library Technology Plans Available Online

Buffalo and Erie County (NY) Public Library Technology Plan 2010-2013
http://bit.ly/14o480C

Cypress College (CA) Library Technology Plan
http://bit.ly/pyQBdR or www.cypresscollege.edu/IRP/Resources/
Accreditation/SSE/IICLibraryLearningSupportServices/
5.16LibraryTechnologyPlan2009-12.pdf

Urbana Free Library Technology Plan (IL)
http://bit.ly/YEf No4

St Charles City-County Library District (MO) Technology Plan
http://bit.ly/oH64co or www.youranswerplace.org/sites/default/files/
ckfinder/files/Tech%20Plan%202012_2014.pdf

Massillon Public Library (OH) Long Range Technology Plan
http://bit.ly/pRvmFF or www.massillonlibrary.org/node/294

with the process, so it might make sense to include a few of them. However, it is important to include different perspectives, so always invite at least one new member to subsequent planning teams.

CONCLUSION

Crafting a technology plan is a significant undertaking that requires a substantial amount of work. However, once the initial plan is complete, subsequent plans will seem easier to do as the process becomes more familiar and documentation for early steps is readily available in former plans. So, take a deep breath. Know you can master the process by following the steps outlined above and using the tools provided throughout the chapter. The online technology plans and the planning resources listed below are a good starting point for your own efforts.

Once you have completed your first technology plan, wave your arms in the air, jump up and down, and tell yourself "I rock!"

LIBRARY TECHNOLOGY PLANNING RESOURCES

Cohn, John M. and Anne L. Kelsey. 2010. *The Complete Library Technology Planner*. New York: Neal-Schuman.

Matthews, Joseph R. 2004. *Technology Planning: Preparing and Updating a Library Technology Plan*. Westport, CT: Libraries Unlimited.

Morrison, Jean V. 2011. *Writing a Winning Technology Plan for E-rate Compliance*. New York: Neal-Schuman.

Writing a Technology Plan in Iowa. http://bit.ly/rrxBf0 or www.statelibraryofiowa.org/ld/e/e-rate/TechPlans.

Writing a Library Technology Plan, Assistance For New Hampshire Libraries. http://1.usa.gov/qrYal9 or www.nh.gov/nhsl/electronic/documents/tech_plan.pdf.

Technology Plan Writing 101 (North Dakota). http://1.usa.gov/q3NydV or www.library.nd.gov/publications/technologyplanwriting101.pdf.

Library Technology Plan Elements (Utah). http://1.usa.gov/oguL7F or http://library.utah.gov/grants/other/plan.html.

Hardware/Software

Rene J. Erlandson

Computer hardware and software are as integral to libraries as books these days. No library operates without a variety of computers and peripherals such as printers and scanners for use by library staff and patrons. The ubiquitous nature of computer technology in our culture is reflected in the ever-increasing number of options available when selecting computer hardware and software. Therefore, rather than being all inclusive, this chapter focuses on ways to manage technology assets and outlines considerations for purchasing hardware and software. Specific hardware and software alternatives useful to libraries are highlighted throughout the chapter.

IT ASSET INVENTORY

Before procuring new hardware and software, it is important to have an accurate inventory of every piece of technology equipment and software (including licenses) owned by the library. While it is tempting to rely on personal memory for this data, an information technology (IT) asset inventory document provides all staff members with up-to-date, detailed information about hardware and software deployments at a glance. Basing acquisitions on a current IT asset inventory will avoid costly duplicate purchases. A simple IT asset inventory can be developed in Excel or another spreadsheet program, by creating a workbook with separate sheets for each category owned by the library: network equipment such as servers

13

and switches; staff computers and public computers; other equipment such as, printers, copiers, scanners, barcode readers, e-readers, and tablets; and software. Detailed information about each piece of equipment or software is recorded within the separate sheets of the workbook. See figure 2.1 for column headings to include on specific sheets of the workbook. Free and low-cost IT asset management software is also available which will automatically inventory all hardware, software, and licenses used on a network. Some packages will even assist in managing an IT help desk and monitor network trouble. Whether you use one of the free asset management packages or create simple spreadsheets with the information, it is important to have an IT asset inventory to refer to when making hardware and software purchasing decisions.

Free and Low-Cost IT Asset Management Software

Lansweeper Network Inventory
www.lansweeper.com

Spiceworks
www.spiceworks.com/product

SysAidIT
www.ilient.com/free-asset-management-software.htm

Network Inventory Advisor
www.clearapps.com

Total Network Inventory & Monitor
www.softinventive.com/products/total-network-inventory

HARDWARE

Outside of collections, hardware is often the most costly investment a library makes, and it is important to realize that hardware does not last forever. Planning is the key to getting the most out of your hardware dollar. The maximum hardware life cycle (i.e., the amount of time hardware is used before it is replaced) is typically thirty-six to forty-eight months. Keep that time frame in mind when considering hardware purchases. One way to mitigate the strain on technology budgets is to implement a sliding hardware replacement cycle, by which a portion of equipment is replaced annually. When 25 percent to 30 percent of technology hardware in the library is replaced annually, the total cost is distributed out over time and new equipment is always available to patrons and staff.

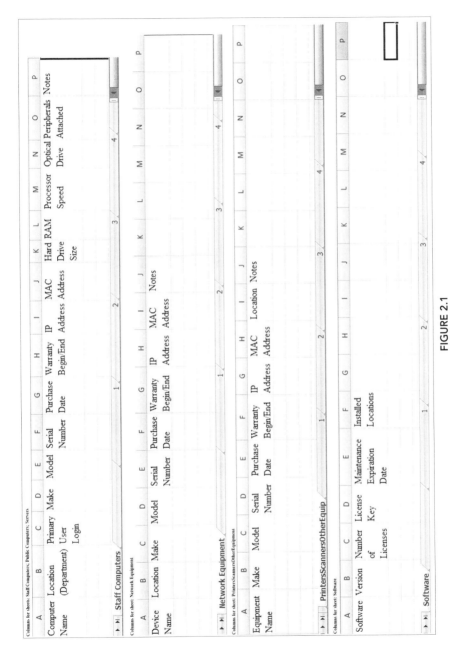

FIGURE 2.1

Sample Column Headings for an IT Asset Inventory Workbook

The decision to purchase hardware should be driven by a specified need: an increase in e-books requests from patrons, inordinate amount of time necessary for staff to render newly created videos, a printer in the public area that stops working. Any of these scenarios may result in the need to purchase new or additional technology equipment. A major mistake to avoid at all costs is purchasing expensive hardware because it is the current fad. For example, purchase an iPad only if it fills an immediate or projected need, not because you want to say the library owns one. Luxury hardware purchases often languish unused on library shelves and result in a missed opportunity to support another technology category.

Whether purchasing new or replacement equipment for staff or public use, think about how hardware will be used immediately and how it will be used throughout its life cycle. For example, before replacing existing workstations consider if they are still a good fit for the library. Do more patrons use their own laptops or mobile devices in the library? If yes, then is the same number of workstations still necessary, or would decreasing the number of workstations free up physical space and technology dollars to be used in other ways? Are circulating laptops checked out to use in the building, even when there are open desktop computer workstations available in the lab? If yes, is this an indicator patrons would prefer to have additional laptops available to check out instead of maintaining existing desktop computer workstations? Are individual staff workstations configured with user-specific software staff would like to use in their office, at the reference desk, or in other areas of the building? If yes, contemplate implementing laptops and docking stations for staff use to facilitate work between locations. By routinely examining how hardware is used and making purchase decisions based on use and need, you can ensure that library technology dollars will be well spent.

IT Asset Management Tips

Create IT asset inventory.

Average hardware life cycle is thirty-six to forty-eight months.

Annually replace 25 percent to 30 percent of hardware.

Desktops and Laptops

When technology hardware is mentioned, desktop computers most often come to mind. However, in the past five years meaningful differences between desktop and laptop computer performance have largely disappeared, thus making laptops viable options to traditional desktop workstations. Therefore, cost and size differences, rather than performance, are often deciding factors for purchasing computers. Desktop workstations still deliver more performance for the money and are less costly to repair. Desktop computer equipment ranges from traditional desktops with large towers to small-form-factor (SFF) desktops. SFF desktops minimize the space needed for the tower, allowing them to be fully installed on top of a desk rather than under the desk or on the floor. When selecting machine features such as memory, processor speed, optical drives, burners, etc., refer to the system requirements for software packages that will be loaded onto the machine and functions the equipment will be used for.

An alternative to standard desktop computers are laptop and docking station configurations. While this arrangement is not standard in public computer labs, it can be useful for staff. When a laptop is docked, it is possible to use a standard monitor, keyboard, mouse, and speakers. However, it is also possible to disconnect the laptop and take it to meetings or other locations to work while retaining complete access to software and clients loaded onto the machine. Laptops range in size from eleven to eighteen inches and vary in weight. As with all computers, consider the types of tasks a laptop will be used for when selecting features. If video conferencing or calling software will be loaded onto the machine, a built-in webcam will be required. If a laptop will be used to watch movies, or listen to audio books, built-in speakers are a must. While webcams and speakers are standard on most laptops, the quality of audio and video will vary, so make sure to purchase a machine that meets your expectations.

Netbooks, Tablets, and e-Readers

Netbooks, tablets, and e-readers are becoming standard equipment in libraries throughout the United States. These lower-cost laptop alternatives increase purchase power for libraries that want to offer flexible, portable access to resources like e-books and streaming media. While not as robust as laptops, these devices support Internet access, standard web browsers, e-readers, streaming media, and simple gaming. Netbooks and tablets also support standard word processing, data management functions, and most available software. Consider the different features of each type of machine and operating system platform before selecting these devices.

Netbooks

A typical netbook has a display screen of ten to ten and a half inches and weighs two to three pounds. Most netbooks have built-in webcams, speakers, and multiple USB hubs to connect to peripherals. Because netbooks are considered mobile devices, they connect to the Internet via wireless, and many do not have network jacks. If an internal network jack is a desired feature, make sure the model being considered has one. Netbooks support most standard software but are not robust enough to efficiently run advanced gaming software and other packages that require significant amounts of RAM and fast processor speeds. In addition, the small keyboard size of netbooks can be uncomfortable for individuals with large hands to use.

Tablets

A tablet is a complete flat-screen mobile computer weighing in at less than one and a half pounds. Tablet touch screens range in size from seven to ten inches and provide high-speed Internet access from hotspots as well as wireless data packages from a variety of mobile service providers. These superthin devices use virtual keyboards, but most can be synced with Bluetooth keyboards for a more traditional configuration if desired. Due to their limited internal storage capacities, tablets are not replacements for laptops or netbooks. However, they are multifunctional alternatives to e-readers. Because Amazon and Barnes & Noble (B&N) have created Kindle and Nook apps for a variety of device platforms including iOS (iPad, iPhone, etc.) and Android, it is possible to use most tablets to access Kindle and Nook e-book purchases as well as PDF and e-pub files. While Kindle and Nook e-book accounts can be registered to iDevices, it is important to note iBook purchases are not viewable on non-iDevices. In addition, as the number of tablets on the market increases it is essential to carefully evaluate each alternative for desired features before purchasing.

e-Readers

Although not as flexible as tablets or as robust as netbooks and laptops, e-readers provide Internet access for web surfing and checking e-mail as well as access to e-books. There are many e-readers available on the market, but the most common are Amazon's Kindle and the Barnes & Noble (B&N) Nook. E-readers range in physical size from six to ten and a half inches, with most weighing in around eight ounces. The Kindle supports PDF and Kindle proprietary files, but not e-pub files. The B&N Nook accesses e-pub files as well as proprietary Nook files. Although PDFs are viewable on the Nook if run through a file converter, they often exhibit formatting issues that can be distracting. None of the e-readers on the market accesses all of the currently used e-book formats. It should also be noted that at the time of publication, B&N offers a Nook that displays color, while Kindle e-readers are grayscale e-ink displays only. In addition, both Amazon and B&N allow one purchased e-book to be loaded onto six devices.

In fall 2011, Amazon announced a partnership with Overdrive to allow public and school libraries to loan Kindle e-books. Users of libraries that subscribe to Overdrive locate Kindle e-books through the local catalog, check the book out with a valid library card, and are then linked to amazon.com to have the book sent wirelessly to the device registered to their Amazon account. Users are able to highlight and bookmark pages within borrowed e-books via the Kindle Whispersync technology. Notations are linked to a user's Amazon account, so if the user checks the book out again, or ultimately purchases the book, the notations are viewable. Although later users never see the notations made by others, Amazon retains the information. When the loan period is up, the book is automatically withdrawn off the device, so late fees are never incurred.

Printers, Copiers, and Scanners

Most libraries offer printing, photocopying, and scanning services to patrons, in addition to staff use. Depending on the configuration of staff work spaces and workflows, stand-alone machines for each activity may be preferential for staff purposes. However, machines that perform all of the tasks may be easier for library patrons to use and more efficient to manage and maintain in public areas. When purchasing this type of equipment, there are a few fundamental considerations to make: how will the equipment be used by the staff and the public? Will the public services be free or fee-based? Is there a need for black-and-white printing only, or will the library need both black-and-white and color printing, copying, and scanning? Will equipment be networked? Are staff capable and willing to maintain and service the equipment? Answering these basic questions will assist in selecting equipment. For more information on selecting scanners see chapter 10.

SOFTWARE

Software refers to computer programs that run on computer hardware. While generally not as expensive as hardware, software programs are still a significant investment for most libraries. Software is often divided into two categories—systems software and applications software. Systems software includes programs that interact to make a computer function, such as operating system and utilities.

Although it is possible to load operating systems, most computers come with standard operating systems and some utilities already loaded. However, some utilities and applications software (e.g., programs designed for end users, such as word processors and spreadsheets) are generally selected and installed by library staff. This section highlights commercial (for fee) and free open-source (FOSS) utilities and application software that are useful to libraries.

Imaging

While no one wants to have a computer crash, at some point it will happen. One way to mitigate the impact of a system malfunction is to create an exact copy of a workstation that can be used to restore the system when needed—a computer image. Windows 7 has a built-in imaging program that can be activated by clicking on the Start icon, typing "backup," and then selecting Backup and Restore. The Windows7 imaging program creates a complete system image that can be used as a backup to reinstall Windows 7 and everything else contained on a workstation, including software and files. If the hard drive of a computer is the primary storage for the workstation, and not a network drive or external hard drive, it is important to frequently create an image that can be used to restore all files if need be. In order to image to network storage, USB, firewire drives, or DVD, use the free edition of Macrium (www.macrium.com/reflectfree.aspx) or Paragon (www.paragon-software .com/home/br-free/download.html). Both of these products create complete system backups that can be used to restore machines via network connections or directly.

Cloning

As anyone who has set up a computer knows, it can take anywhere from a couple of hours to all day to install the operating system, drivers, and software on one workstation. However, cloning, also known as ghosting, reduces setup time for multiple workstations by replicating installed operating system, drivers, and desired software packages from a single computer. Clonezilla SE (http://clonezilla.org/clonezilla-SE) is a free and open-source cloning software that can clone about forty computers at a time, while Symantec Ghost (www.symantec.com/business/ghost-solution-suite) is a commercial product that can deploy hundreds of Windows-based clones in a matter of minutes. Depending on budget and support needed, either package is a viable option for managing deployments in computer lab environments.

Anti-virus and Anti-malware

Every computer used by the public or that connects to the Internet needs to be protected from programs that can invade a workstation and cause a system malfunction, gather personal information, or allow unauthorized access to system resources. There are a plethora of malicious programs unleashed on the Internet that can be unwittingly downloaded onto a computer with the click of a mouse. Depending on the program, once in a system it is possible for a malicious program to infect an entire network. Therefore it is critical to protect every machine in the library, as much as possible, from these attacks.

Anti-virus software is designed to detect and destroy computer viruses, while anti-malware identifies and blocks a variety of malicious programs, including spyware, Trojan horses, worms, and rootkits. Before downloading any anti-virus or anti-malware software from the Internet, make sure it originates from a reputable source. Many Trojan horses masquerade as anti-virus programs, only to unleash viruses into a system upon executing. One of the most common commercial antivirus software packages available is Norton AntiVirus (http://us.norton.com). ClamWin (www.clamwin.com/content/view/18/46) and Avast (www.avast.com/en-us/index) are free reputable antivirus alternatives. In addition, Malwarebytes Anti-Malware (www.malwarebytes.org) offers an effective free edition that supports multiple drive scanning (including network drives) and scan-on-demand of individual files for a variety of malicious programs. Like many other programs that started out as anti-virus software, ClamAV (www.clamav.net/lang/en) now offers anti-malware protection, including anti-virus. Regardless of which software is used, the importance of installing this type of security on public lab machines cannot be overemphasized.

Hardware Protection

Another way to eliminate malware issues on public computer stations or circulating equipment like laptops is to install software that protects the hard drive by returning the computer to predetermined settings and configurations upon every reboot. Commercial software programs such as Deep Freeze (www.faronics.com/enterprise/deep-freeze) prevent unauthorized changes from being permanently saved on the hard drive of a computer by creating a snapshot of a workstation's configuration and settings and then returning the workstation to the authorized configuration every time the machine is rebooted. Centurion Technologies (www.centuriontech .com) and Fortres Grand Clean Slate (www.fortresgrand.com/products/cls/cls.htm) offer workstation management solutions that provide log-on security and disk protection through restore-to-reboot as well as restoration upon each new log-in. Both Centurion and Clean Slate also provide avenues for software deployment and asset inventory for an all-in-one asset management package.

Print Management

As the cost of paper, toner, and ink cartridges increased, most libraries made the decision to limit printing or pass along printing costs to library users. Many libraries today rely on print management software to manage printing quotas or collect fees from users. Antamedia Print Manager (www.antamedia.com/print-manager) and Software Shelf Print Manager Plus are commercial software packages that provide free trial downloads to test out each system. License bundles for Antamedia range from $99 (to manage two printers) up to $599 (for an unlimited number of printers). Other commercial products include Pharos Print Optimization & Management (www.pharos.com/library/library-solutions-overview.html) and GoPrint (www.goprint.com/products.html) that work with libraries to implement pay-for-print/copy services and mobile printing. Columbia University's NINJa is a free, open-source option available at (www.columbia.edu/acis/dev/projects/ninja) but requires a significant amount of configuration and setup.

Productivity Applications

While commercial packages like MS Office and Adobe Creative Suites are widely known, some of the free productivity applications are less common to end users. Two such suites are OpenOffice (www.openoffice.org) and LibreOffice (www .libreoffice.org). Both packages run on Windows or Macintosh platforms and include word processing, spreadsheet, presentation, database, and image applications. GIMP (www.gimp.org), a free image manipulation program that allows users to compose and author images, convert image formats, and retouch photos and works on both Windows and Mac platforms, is a free alternative to Adobe Photoshop.

Child-Friendly Search and Web Filtering

For libraries that serve children, special search and filtering software may be required or desired. Google SafeSearch (www.safesearchkids.com), Kid Clicks (www.kidclicks.org), and Ask Kids (http://sp.askkids.com/docs/askkids/index .shtml) are just a sampling of the free kid-friendly search engines available. There are also a plethora of web filters available to libraries and schools. Net Nanny (www.netnanny.com/login) offers free trial downloads of ContentProtect to librar- ies and schools to test the software before purchasing. K9 Web Protection (www1. k9webprotection.com/#organization) begins pricing at $12.49 per year per license. Always check with local, regional, and statewide library agencies and consortia to discover if your library can use existing resources or qualifies as a member for bulk orders of this type of software.

HARDWARE AND SOFTWARE COST SAVINGS

As previously mentioned, hardware and software purchases are expensive, so every dollar saved is a dollar that can be spent elsewhere. Do not be afraid to contact vendor sales representatives directly. It is often possible to negotiate a better deal directly than to simply accept online or local prices. Savings may be possible if you are purchasing more than one or two pieces of the same equipment or software packages. Many vendors, such as Dell and Canon, will give discounts on purchases of as few as three machines of the same model. In addition, when purchasing multiple pieces of equipment, it is often possible to negotiate for maintenance or service agreements and extended warranties at reduced or no cost.

When purchasing software, look for bundled packages that include multiple programs. Software vendors often bundle popular or task-related programs together at substantially reduced prices. Choosing to purchase a license key that allows software to be downloaded rather than requesting software programs on physical media like CD-ROMs can also reap cost savings. In addition, some software licenses allow for purchased programs to be downloaded on multiple machines used by the same individual. So, if purchasing software for a staff member who uses a desktop workstation and a laptop, it may be possible to purchase one license and deploy it to both work-related computers.

CONCLUSION

Diligent planning and investigation are the keys to making successful hardware and software selections. Creating and maintaining an IT asset inventory will aid in spending technology dollars wisely. Carefully examining current equipment uses and considering future functions and needs are the cornerstones of hardware and software selection decisions. Add to this strategy working with affiliated agencies and vendors to get the best possible bargain on equipment and using open-source, low-cost, or bundled software and you are well on your way to taming the technology dragon.

Infrastructure / Networking

Scott Childers

Networking is the connecting together of computers to share files and resources. You may want to set up a network so everyone in the office can share a printer or work on documents without bouncing them around in e-mail. Networks can be wired or wireless. Both methods have their strengths and weaknesses. Wired is often more stable and usually faster, but the user is tethered to a cable. Wireless allows greater flexibility but can be less stable and possibly slower. Networking using either method can be simple or very complex. This chapter will highlight simple networking methods often suggested for home use, but that will work well for small libraries.

WIRED NETWORKING

Wired networking is the traditional method of connecting a computer through Ethernet cabling, using servers, hubs, switches, and file sharing. A wired network can be created fairly simply for a small number of computers using a few simple options, or it can be quite complex with more features for a larger number of computers.

This chapter will concentrate on LANs, or local area networks. LANs are defined as a network constrained by a limited physical area, like a single building. WANs, or wide area networks, are outside the scope of this book in which they cover multiple areas.

Another item of note is that this chapter will not include detailed information on integrating Internet access into the local network. Adding Internet access to an existing network requires service from a local Internet service provider and a piece of hardware called a router. Routers are affordable and are often built in as part of a multiple function device, such as a wireless access point and router combination.

Servers

The term *server* can be used in a variety of ways when talking about computers. For this chapter, servers are defined as computers that serve a special function in a network. Servers house data, files, or even programs that are accessible to all computers on the network. They also provide for many services such as user authentication.

Hubs and Switches

A *hub* is a device that routes network traffic between machines. All computers on the network have an Ethernet cable that connects to a hub which continuously sends traffic to all computers on the network.

A *switch* is similar to a hub, but it has one important distinction. A switch only sends traffic to the machine it is directed to. For example, if user A wants to access files on computer B, a switch sends the request directly only to computer B instead of broadcasting it across the entire network. A switch is therefore much more efficient when routing traffic, resulting in better overall network speed. For many years, it was also the more expensive option, but switches are now cheaper than they used to be and probably the better option for most networks.

How to Set Up a LAN

One of the first decisions you need to make is the overall model of network you want to implement. There are two main types of models: the client-server model and the peer-to-peer model. Both have their strengths and weaknesses. You could also set up your network using a hybrid of the two. For example: my computer at work is connected to the network using the client-server model; a central shared space is available for our files. However, the printer attached to my computer is shared with an office mate's computer in a peer-to-peer setup.

Client-Server

Using a client-server methodology of networking means you are using a central computer to direct traffic and store files. Each computer on the network is connected to a central server, as shown in figure 3.1. Files are stored on this server and can be accessed by any other computer on the network. In some cases, everything is done on the server and the user has only one program, the client, which collects input and distributes outputs. This method has more of an up-front cost in time and money and requires more maintenance, but is easier to scale up as you add more computers to the network. If you chose to use this method, you should consider hiring a professional.

Peer-to-Peer

A peer-to-peer network skips the central server and instead has each computer sharing resources directly with each other, as shown in figure 3.2. If a user needs a resource on a certain computer, the user connects to that computer directly. That also means if the needed computer is powered down or otherwise removed from the network, resources attached to that computer are unavailable. This method is easier to set up and is suggested for a small library.

27

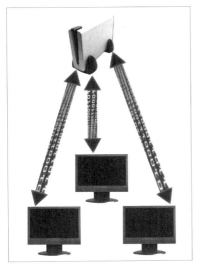

FIGURE 3.1
Client-Server Network
Configuration

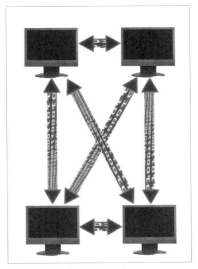

FIGURE 3.2
Peer-to-Peer Network
Configuration

By using a hub, a switch, or a crossover cable that allows you to connect two computers directly, you can connect all the computers. That takes care of the physical part of networking. Next is the software step. Depending on the type of computers you are using, there is most likely a network wizard available that will walk you through the steps of creating a network. For connecting staff computers in a small library, you may consider using the home network or workgroup options. Follow the steps of the wizard, and then on each computer choose which file directories or peripherals are shared with the rest of the network.

Creating a Firewall

A firewall is a piece of security software that is used to block incoming and outgoing network traffic. You can use a firewall to block certain ports, certain pieces of software, or individual protocols. Firewalls can be instituted on the individual computer or at the server level. If you are running a peer-to-peer network, then the firewalls should be activated on each machine. Windows has a firewall system built in and it will suffice in most instances. Your router, hub, or switch may also have firewall capabilities built in.

WIRELESS NETWORKING

Wireless networking is exactly as it sounds: networking using wireless technology. This has an advantage over wired networks because there are fewer total cables and increased mobility. Connectivity is achieved by having a device called a wireless access point, otherwise known as a WAP. You could have multiple access points that relay wirelessly between themselves to spread the coverage of the Wi-Fi network. To attach the Wi-Fi network to the Internet you eventually have to connect to a router that is connected to your Internet source to spread the connection throughout the building. You can purchase a router that has both a wireless access point and an Ethernet hub or switch built in, allowing you to set up both a wired and wireless network using one device. For a small physical location this is a great solution.

Wi-Fi comes with a price because wireless bandwidth is shared with everyone else who is attached to the access point. When several devices are actively using the network at the same time, the connections slow down for everyone. There are also some security issues that will be presented later in the chapter.

Wireless LAN

Like the wired LAN, a wireless LAN can be made in different ways. A peer-to-peer model, similar to the model of the same name in wired networking, can be created by wireless devices talking directly to each other. This method is used mostly for ad hoc networking and not so much for a long-term networking solution. A better, long-term solution will be talked about after some basic security discussion. See the resources listed at the end of this chapter for additional information on setting up small networks.

Wireless Security

Security for a wireless LAN is important because many of the default settings on wireless access points are wide open. The network traffic can be picked up by any interested third party who invests in some relatively accessible hardware or software. Encryption and strong passwords are mandatory for any staff-only wireless networks.

Encryption

Normally traffic over a Wi-Fi connection is sent in plain text, and anyone who is within the radius of the Wi-Fi network can possibly intercept the information. Encryption is used to code the traffic so only devices that have the right encryption set can see what it really is. This discourages sniffing by making it harder to grab information. There are different types of encryption available for wireless security, but Wi-Fi Protected Access (WPA) encryption is the suggested minimum. The previous system, WEP or Wired Equivalent Privacy, has been found to have serious weaknesses.

Password

Having a strong password is recommended to prevent easy access for unauthorized users. However, if you have a strong password but give it away to everyone who asks, then it is worthless.

How to Set Up a Wi-Fi Network

When setting up a Wi-Fi network the first thing you need to examine is the building itself. The size of the space is not the only determinant of how effective a

29

wireless router or access point would be. The materials and obstacles the signals have to go through could also have an effect. Does your building have walls made of drywall, or are they concrete block? Do you have really tall shelves full of books, or are they only waist high? Different materials have different effects on the signal, and the obstacles wireless signals have to go through can reduce the effective range of a wireless router. If you are just starting out, you might want to install your router temporarily in one location and plan on moving it occasionally to see what location gives you the best coverage. You might also think about adding access points to spread the signal to places on the fringe of your access point's signal.

Once you get your access point running, you should go into the control panel to set some security adjustments. You will have to check the manual of your access point, but you usually are given a specific IP number to type into your web browser. This lets you change things about your network, like the name of the network, encryption levels, and more. It is strongly suggested you change both the name of the network and the password for the control panel.

Changing the name of the network has two advantages. First, it allows you to broadcast it as "such-and-such library" instead of a default name like Linksys. This makes it easier for users to know this is the library's wireless network, not a neighbor's. Second, it adds a small amount of security to your network. It shows that this particular network isn't using default settings, and there may be easier pickings down the line. Changing the default password is also a good idea because the factory-set passwords for access points and routers are easily found and used. This password is the password for access point's control panel, not the network encryption password.

Now that you have set up the access point and changed the security settings, you can add wireless devices to the network. Start up the device to be added and locate the network. Set up the encryption method as you set it up in the control panel. The device should now be able to access the network.

You have to balance security versus ease of access. If you are creating a wireless network for your patrons, you may have to have a less secure network. The more secure you make it, the more time your staff will spend helping patrons get on the network. Some places will have two Wi-Fi networks: one that is very secure for staff who would have known devices, and a second, less-secure network for the public to easily access with their electronic devices.

EXPLANATION OF CLOUD COMPUTING

Those who promote cloud computing pay it great worth, but definitions are often hard to come by. Cloud computing is probably best described as using remote computers to do work and return results to local computers. Remote and local are also terms that depend on your point of view. For example, let's say you are running a server in your own library that runs your online catalog. For you, in your building, you probably wouldn't consider it cloud computing because you maintain the server. However, your patrons accessing it from their homes would probably consider this cloud computing because the work is being done somewhere other than where they are. Libraries have actually been using facets of cloud computing for years in the form of online databases, and some are subscribing to cloud-based integrated library systems. People often refer to storing files in the cloud as well. This is a related term that denotes using some remote server to store files, accessing them through the Internet as needed.

Why and When You Might Choose Cloud Computing

An organization may choose a cloud computing option for many reasons. There are free web-based options for many things you need to do. These include web-based word processing and spreadsheets like Google docs and e-mail providers like Gmail, Yahoo mail, and Windows Live. For small organizations, these provide adequate tools with no cost and no need for high-end computers or local servers. There are also subscription services available that still might be cheaper than housing a local installation of a program. For example, the Seward Memorial Library in Seward, Nebraska, went from a locally hosted integrated library system to subscribing to a cloud-based system for a savings of approximately $1,000 per year; another $2,000 was saved by not having to buy a replacement server. Another example is the University of Nebraska Lincoln Libraries' decision to subscribe to a cloud-based product for creating online subject guides instead of choosing a similar locally hosted product for which they would have had to pay yearly licensing costs, as well as the hidden cost of maintaining the system itself, which would have included staff time, electricity, cooling, and training.

How Cloud Computing Affects Local Networking

Using cloud-based programs can affect local networking dramatically if there are many users at the same time. There will be a constant need for network bandwidth when using cloud-based programming and storage, so the network needs to be stable and fast. That is the trade-off you make to use web-based programs: reduced need for local storage and servers but increased need for network bandwidth, both wired and wireless.

CONCLUSION

Setting up a computer network for a small physical space can be done easily and affordably using equipment found at a local computer store or online. Creating a simple peer-to-peer network using a modern operating system's built-in networking wizard is sufficient for most small libraries' networking needs.

Wireless networks can be set up just as easily for small spaces. Remember to secure your wireless network with proper encryption and good password policies.

Cloud computing resources can help you make the most of your networked setup, allowing you universal access to applications, file storage, and more. The trade-off is that your network and Internet connection will be used more and may cause some speed reduction.

NETWORKING RESOURCES

Apple. 2010. "Creating a Small Ethernet Network." March. http://support.apple.com/kb/ht1433.

Bing, Benny. 2000. *High-Speed Wireless ATM and LANS*. Boston: Artech House.

Microsoft. 2011. "5 steps: How to Set Up Your Home Wireless Network." *Microsoft at Home*. www.microsoft.com/athome/organization/wirelesssetup.aspx.

Muller, Nathan J. 2003. *LANs to WANs: The Complete Management Guide*. Boston: Artech House.

Palmer, Michael J. and Robert Bruce Sinclair. 1999. *A Guide to Designing and Implementing Local and Wide Area Networks*. Toronto: Course Technology.

Rist, Oliver and Eric Griffith. 2009. "Home Networking in 5 Easy Steps." *PC Magazine*, March 16. www.pcmag.com/article2/0,2817,2343082,00.asp.

Integrated Library Systems

Rachel A. Erb

B efore you decide whether it is necessary for your library to have an integrated library system, it is imperative that you understand the basics of an ILS. A quick keyword search using Google will result in an overwhelming array of definitions. As a former systems librarian, I would define an ILS as a relational database that performs various functions such as cataloging, acquisitions, and serial check-in through the use of discrete modules for specific operations. How about a broader definition? Tristan Muller offers: "Integrated library systems (ILS) are multifunction, adaptable software applications that allow libraries to manage, catalog, and circulate their materials to patrons."

The definition of an ILS has changed over time with the evolution of technology. At this moment there are ILS functions that might have defied prediction twenty years ago: global updating of bibliographic records, resource sharing, graphical interfaces, and support for web-based online catalogs, to name just a few. Therefore, it is essential to have the most current understanding while remaining aware that further change is inevitable.

FUNCTIONAL REQUIREMENTS OF AN ILS

There are several basic functions of an ILS.

- Expedite and eliminate current manual functions.
- Search among various record types.

- Permit the creation and enhancement of databases.
- Manage budget and finances, eliminating the need for spreadsheets.
- Provide connectivity to the Internet and web server hosting for an online catalog.
- Create graphical user interfaces.
- Provide powerful and sophisticated front- and back-end search algorithms.
- Provide access to and manage materials in a variety of formats.
- Support several types of metadata schema (MARC, XML, etc.).
- Provide thorough documentation and/or technical support.
- Ensure adaptability for future technological innovations.

LIBRARY FACILITIES AND STAFFING

The sheer number of propriety and open-source (OS) integrated library systems increases each year. While products from big name vendors such as Innovative, Sirsi, and Ex Libris are some of the top choices among libraries with ample budgets, you are likely reading this chapter because these products are too expensive for your library. Not to worry—there are many low-cost alternatives that can assist with your library's operations. But even when we eliminate the larger players in the ILS world, selecting a low-cost alternative requires careful planning. First, be able to articulate a broad picture of the library. If possible, form a comprehensive ILS review team with representatives from every department of your library and begin the conversation as a unified group. Here are a few things to consider:

- Type of library
- Size of collection
- Budget
- Staff size
- Skill level of staff
- Network and server management (on-site versus off-site)
- Availability of high-speed Internet
- Future technology goals of the library
- Formats the collection comprises now and will comprise in the next few years—monographs, serials, artwork, e-resources, digital images, etc.

Take copious notes during these meetings. Write more detail than is probably necessary, as these notes will prove essential when you begin to draft an RFP (request for proposal). The RFP process will be discussed in more detail later in this chapter.

Once the review team has a firm picture of the library's role and its future direction, it should identify desired functions that reflect the current and anticipated future needs of the library. Here are some specific questions to facilitate decision making.

- What specific functions should be automated?
- Will any items circulate?
- What features are critical to streamline staff workloads?
- Does the library need an acquisitions module to manage orders, funds, and budgets? What are the essential functions of the acquisitions module that are required to improve current fiscal operations?
- Describe how the library is technologically supported. What is the level of IT support in the library?
- Which metadata schema is necessary (MARC, XML, etc.)? Consider the staff's readiness to migrate to RDA and if the new system supports it.
- Is it essential that the ILS host an online catalog? How much flexibility is desired to configure the look and feel of the online catalog?
- What type of searching will you want for the online catalog (keyword, title, author, journal title, subject)?
- Are electronic resources a substantial part of the library's collection? Does the library anticipate future growth in that area? If so, must the ILS have the capability to manage them?
- How many simultaneous users are needed to use the ILS? What is the estimated number of simultaneous users for the online catalog?
- Does the library want a secure system that provides daily back of up of data?
- Will digital images be included?

These questions do not represent an exhaustive list, but they will engender further discussion questions and topics. Keep discussions focused and proceed in a timely manner. Technology discussions generally evoke a whole host of emotions in people, so it is imperative to maintain a healthy level of optimism when leading these discussions. Having a realistic picture of current and future technological needs will assist in compiling a reasonable list of desired ILS features. This will also prevent purchasing a system that is too robust for the library's needs. This is detrimental and not cost effective. For example, if your library collects mostly electronic journals and only a few specialized databases and has no plans to divert from this path within the next few years, it is not crucial that your ILS handle digital formats.

After several meetings, it is likely that a list of requirements will emerge. It is important these are identified early in the selection process, prior to reviewing specific ILS products. Realistically, there is no one ideal ILS, but there exists a close match to any library's functional requirements.

Before exploring vendor options, it is prudent to determine if there are any consortia your library could join. Many are based on library type. For example, the South Carolina Information and Library Services is a consortium of community colleges of varying sizes throughout the state. Joining a consortium could save the library money, and the ability to work with peer libraries is invaluable. If the consortium option does not exist, then it is time to investigate vendors.

ILS VENDOR INVESTIGATION

Now that the review team has an idea of the functional requirements, it is time to investigate ILS products and vendors. Many vendors specialize in offering an ILS based on the type of library. There are also vendor-hosted, open-source alternatives that many small libraries are using for a nominal fee. Finding appropriate vendors can present a challenge, but there are various ways to identify ones that are suitable. If it is possible to attend one of the national association conferences such as ALA, SLA, or PLA, the vendor exhibition hall will allow you to meet with various vendor representatives in one location. For many of us working in small or solo operations, conference attendance might not be feasible. Fortunately, there is a comprehensive resource online, Library Technology Guide (www.librarytech nology.org) that contains objective information regarding industry news, library companies, and a directory of live library catalogs. The site also offers a historical chart of library vendors. Another website, WebJunction (www.webjunction.org/ ils), provides an ILS selection guide.

Once the team has a list of prospective vendors, it is time to research some of the particulars regarding vendors to hone in on ones that potentially suit your library's needs:

- Does the vendor specialize in your type of library? Are there other vendors that can still be considered although they do not specialize in your type of library?
- How current is the vendor's ILS development? Is there evidence that the vendor is investing in future development? For example, what modules are under development?

- Are there any annual maintenance fees? If so, do they fit the library's budget?
- What is the vendor's overall plan to meet the demands of emerging technologies that are relevant to your library?
- How is the vendor's customer service? A good way to find out is to ask for references and contact several of them.
- How many new subscribers have there been within the past two years? Are any of them similar to your library?
- What is the financial outlook of the vendor? In the current climate of mergers and acquisitions, it is really important that the company is financially stable and has a promising future. A vendor buyout could force a migration to another ILS upon your library at the wrong time. Request a current financial report from the vendor.
- Is there assistance with implementation? Training? Ongoing training for new and advanced features once it is launched?
- How are upgrades handled?
- Is there a turnkey option or is the library responsible for hosting the software?
- What modules are available? Are there any add-on modules (often with additional costs, so be sure to check!) that are standard in other systems?
- How long will it take for the vendor to install the system?
- What do the warranties cover?
- What type of platform (cloud, client-server, standalone)?

37

MATCHING MANUAL WORKFLOWS WITH ILS WORKFLOWS

It is time to examine existing workflows and determine how the workflow will fit with the prospective integrated library systems. Creating flowcharts of current processes will assist with this endeavor. There are some excellent free flowchart programs available, such as Lucidchart, (www.lucidchart.com). Focus on the specific functionalities of each ILS on the short list and determine how the current manual processes are handled by the ILS. Create additional flowcharts specifying the ILS functions whenever possible.

REQUEST FOR PROPOSAL (RFP)

A request for proposal (RFP) is a formal document asking for bids for a product and service. The library prepares an RFP in order to obtain a customized proposal from a vendor. The RFP must enumerate the library's needs.

Writing an RFP is not for the faint of heart. Fortunately, there are numerous free online resources. A good place to begin is the *RFP Writer's Guide to Standards for Library Systems* (www.niso.org/publications/press/RFP_Writers_Guide.pdf), published by the National Information Standards Organization. There are also plenty of sample RFPs available as well. Use them as models to make sure you include all the necessary elements. In general, be prepared to write a narrative of the library's background, its mission statement, technology plan, and network operating system. Sound familiar? Yes, this is all the information the ILS team discussed prior to getting to this stage. (See, there was a purpose for those meetings!)

Once the RFP is drafted it is time to submit the document to prospective vendors for review. Expect a response that will include pricing, implementation plan, and timeline. The vendor's response initiates the negotiation process, so be prepared to meet with them either face-to-face or virtually.

MEETING WITH VENDORS

Prior to meeting with vendors, meet with the ILS implementation team and agree upon a list of questions. Request a demonstration of the system's modules either in person or via webcast. In some cases, you may be able to receive a demo account. Have staff either attend these sessions or, when possible, test the products themselves. The demonstration period will engender more questions. Gauge how responsive the prospective vendor is when answering these questions. Are the answers satisfactory? The vendor-client relationship is an integral part of the subscription life span. Make sure it is one that will meet your library's needs now and in the future.

PURCHASING AND BEYOND

Once the ILS team decides to purchase a particular ILS, there are costs involved with maintenance throughout the life of the system. Many vendors implement an annual software maintenance service charge. In addition, there are upgrades, add-on modules, etc.—all designed to maximize the ILS's potential, adding to the total cost of the system. As the ILS changes over time, training needs of staff will arise. Perhaps there are user group conferences that staff will wish to participate in as part of their continuing education. Be sure to account for these ongoing issues when making budgetary projections.

NO FORMAL PROCESS NECESSARY

Some small libraries do not require a formalized, extensive selection process and therefore will not have to submit an RFP to vendors. In these instances, the library needs an ILS that is simple to implement and requires little to no IT support. Many of these libraries will seek either open-source or low-cost ILS alternatives.

A WORD ABOUT OPEN SOURCE

If you think that libraries have to forgo open-source integrated library systems because there is a lack of IT support and staff programming skills, think again. An emerging trend is vendor-hosted ILSs, otherwise known as software-as-a-service (SaaS). Offering an ILS as SaaS eliminates the burden of the library having to maintain the product. Open-source ILSs are defined as those requiring installation and self-hosting. The vendor is responsible for all aspects of technical support: installation, upgrades, troubleshooting, and so forth. For small and solo library operations it is imperative to investigate open-source ILS options that have a high level of support.

One caveat to bear in mind is that open-source ILS vendor support is not free. There are either annual or monthly subscription fees. In many cases, the fees are manageable for more limited budgets, currently around $1,000 or less per year. Ideally, one would prefer a free web-based ILS, but this does not currently exist. The current ILS climate, especially with the advent of OCLC's Web-scale Management Services in 2010, suggests that it is only a matter of time before a similar open-source product offering a web-based ILS is readily available.

Another consideration is that proprietary systems developed over many years generally have more advanced features. The library must determine if the open-source ILS "has achieved a high enough level of functionality" and "if the development models in place will result in an adequate pace of advancement" (Breeding 2007). Many small and solo operations can probably find an open-source ILS that meets their needs.

SOME LOW-COST ALTERNATIVES

There are several low-cost SaaS integrated library systems available for a subscription fee. This is not meant to be an exhaustive list, but an overview of some of the more popular options. The key features of each ILS will be highlighted, but it is recommended that the reader use this section as a starting point and further investigate each product.

LibraryWorld ($395 per year)

Used by more than 2,000 libraries, LibraryWorld is an uncomplicated SaaS ILS that offers modules for a library's core functions. These functions include the following:

- LibraryWorld OPAC—web-based online catalog
- Catalog with an interface for a mobile device
- Cataloging (import MARC records from the Library of Congress or perform original cataloging)
- Circulation
- Patron management
- Inventory
- Printing of reports and spine or pocket labels
- Administration (controls individual authorizations within the system)

LibraryWorld is ideal for a small collection consisting of all formats. It is possible to demo this product with a thirty-day trial to determine if it is suitable for your library. This ILS is very basic, but there are some more advanced functions such as global updating and exporting records. Recently, LibraryWorld began to allow catalog searches via a mobile device. The absence of an acquisitions module may be a potential drawback for some libraries, but one that can be overcome if the library has a very small collections budget.

ResourceMate ($195)

ResourceMate is very inexpensive and offers a core level of ILS functionalities. Because it is not as robust as other systems, the application is ideal for smaller collections (fewer than10,000 items).

The system offers several basic functionalities:

- Cataloging—retrieve MARC records from the Library of Congress and others with Z39.50 servers via ISBN
- Circulation
- Web-based online catalog

- Reports—shelf lists, overdue items, etc.
- Label printing—spine labels, etc.

It is possible to upgrade ResourceMate with several add-on modules that sell for between $99 and $195 each. These add-on modules include an advanced circulation feature that allows customization of loan rules, a bookings feature for equipment reservations, and web searching for the online catalog.

ResourceMate currently offers subscribers technical support for free during the first free months of the subscription. After this initial period, support is currently billed at $70 per year.

OPALS (Open-Source Automated Library System) ($500–$600)

OPALS is an open-source, web-based ILS that is used by a wide variety of libraries: school, college, business, and religious organizations. OPALS is also employed as a union catalog for interlibrary loan services. OPALS's varied functionalities within each module are impressive, even rivaling some commercial analogs.

The modules include the following functionalities:

- Public access catalog (OPAC)
- Cataloging—MARC records are imported from any Z39.50 server of your choosing.
- Circulation
- Inventory
- Administration
- Reports/notices—circulation statistics, overdue notices, etc.
- Interlibrary loan management—basic interlibrary loan software functions: requests, responses, printouts, and tracking

Technical support will set up a trial by creating an evaluation site with uploaded MARC bibliographic records from your library. During this time, prospective clients will be able to ask technical support staff any questions they may have or obtain additional assistance using any of the modules. The user documentation from OPALS's website is comprehensive. The developers also list current users of this system, and this is useful for contacting subscribers for references. The developers also offer comprehensive technical support—from getting started to troubleshooting.

Koha Express ($300–$900)

Koha Express is a subscription-based, turnkey ILS that is hosted on LibLime's cloud platform. The subscription rate includes technical support and automatic upgrades to the system as new releases are made available. LibLime offers three add-on features that facilitate data migration, training, and OPAC customization.

Koha's features:

- Automated voice message for patrons regarding overdue fees and items on hold
- Ability to create and share booklists with other users
- Reporting
- Community tagging
- Integrated Z39.50 client with cataloging module
- Basic acquisitions system
- RSS (Really Simple Syndication) feeds for search results
- Zotero integration

As part of the first generation of open-source integrated library systems, Koha is a more mature system than others, and enhancement is continuous. The detailed and copious documentation regarding Koha's functionalities indicate continual technological development of this product. If your library collection is small (fewer than 75,000 bibliographic records), but robust features are essential, then Koha Express is ideal. There are two potential drawbacks to Koha Express: unlike Koha, data migration costs extra and technical support via telephone is excluded. Despite these minor limitations, Koha Express has the same functionalities as Koha.

THE FUTURE OF THE ILS

The current technological trend of software-as-a-service available in the cloud will continue to influence how ILSs are enhanced. While this trend will resolve some key issues such as maintaining upgrades and server hosting, a fatal flaw still persists: Marshall Breeding aptly suggests that the current roster of ILSs does not match the workflows of today's libraries. The ILS was adequate when print was the predominant format managed in libraries, but now print is being eclipsed by digital content. At the same time, integrated library systems still contain many features that reflect a level of automation from twenty-five years ago. This struggle is borne out in current workflows, where "far too much time is spent on getting systems to work at the expense of more fruitful activity" (Pace 2007, 649). A solution, however, is not a remote possibility because "the software needs to be designed around the processes and tasks that meet the goals of the organization" (Breeding 2007). Since 2007, ILSs have evolved in this direction. It is likely that this will be the future trajectory of ILS, but no one can predict the future.

The current state of the ILS, coupled with an uncertain future, is cold comfort for those operating small and solo libraries. Managing these types of libraries entails myriad responsibilities, so it can be difficult to remain aware of ILS trends and issues.

INTEGRATED LIBRARY SYSTEMS

Hodgson, Cynthia. 2002. *RFP Writer's Guide to Standards for Library Systems.* Bethesda, MD: National Information Standards Organization. (www .niso.org/publications/press/ RFP_Writers_Guide.pdf).

Library Technology Guides. (http://librarytechnology.org).

American Library Association. 2011. "Negotiating Contracts with Integrated Library System Vendors." October 10. (www.ala.org/pla/tools/technotes/negotiatingils).

Webber, Desiree and Andrew Peters. 2010. *Integrated Library Systems: Planning, Selecting, and Implementing.* Westport, CT: Libraries Unlimited.

WebJunction (www.webjunction.org/ils).

REFERENCES

Breeding, Marshall. 2007. "It's Time to Break the Mold of the Original ILS." *Computers in Libraries,* November/December. www.librarytechnology.org/ltg-displaytext .pl?RC=12881.

Pace, Andrew. 2009. "21st Century Library Systems." *Journal of Library Administration* 49, no. 6: 641–650.

PART 2

e-Resources

Fundamentals of Electronic Resources

Rachel A. Erb

The increase in the number of e-resources (electronic resources) added to library collection over the past fifteen years has significantly impacted collection development, even among the smallest of libraries. During that time, library budgets were marked by a steep decline in allocating funds for print mterials in favor of electronic formats. E-resources encompass a wide variety of materials, including journals, books, indexes, reference books, full-text and partial full-text databases, electronic texts sorted in institutional repositories, white and gray papers, federal and state depository resources, and aggregator databases that collect full-text journals from different publishers. While larger research and public libraries are able to absorb this change with greater, more flexible budgets, acquiring and managing electronic resources may be a challenge for smaller libraries. This chapter will assist with the reader's foray into e-resource collection development and management.

SELECTION OF E-RESOURCES: WHERE TO BEGIN

Selecting e-resources to add to the library's collection is less complicated if there is a collection development policy in place. Minimally, this policy should articulate the library's mission, identify the community served, and address when e-resources should be selected instead of print materials and vice versa. It cannot be overemphasized that you must be proactive in understanding what your users need before you begin writing a collection development policy. Library type will dictate the stakeholders. School librarians should solicit input from teachers and administration to ensure the resources will meet curriculum needs. Librarians at small academic libraries must regularly reach out to faculty, and stay abreast of new majors. Public librarians must know their user community and work with library boards to determine how to build an electronic collection. Even though librarians at special libraries often have a narrow mission and, consequently, a monolithic user community, they need to determine which e-resources will enhance their small, but valuable collection.

While it is beyond the scope of this chapter to instruct the reader on the composition of a collection development policy, there are some excellent resources that target smaller libraries.

Arizona State Library—Collection Development Training
www.lib.az.us/cdt/intro.aspx

OWLSWeb—Sample Policies for the Small Public Library
www.owlsweb.info/L4L/policies/VIII.asp

IFLA—Guidelines for a Collection Development Policy
http://archive.ifla.org/VII/s14/nd1/gcdp-e.pdf

ALA—Collection Development
www.ala.org/ala/professionalresources/atoz/Collection
%20Development/collectiondevelopment.cfm

Medical Library Association (MLA)
http://colldev.mlanet.org/resources/professional_resources
.htm#colldevpols

National Information Standards Organization (NISO). A Framework
of Guidance for Building Good Digital Collections
http://framework.niso.org

Once its collection development policy is completed, it will be easier for the library to select appropriate e-resources that are in concert with the policy. It is not, however, a simple matter. The proliferation of e-resources makes selection a unique challenge. How does one decide which e-resources to include in the library's collection—especially within the confines of a modest budget? Fortunately, there are many resources to assist with selection. Most of the resources listed here are free, but some require paid subscriptions and will be duly noted.

Electronic Mailing List Servers (Listservs)

The listservs listed below can help with electronic resource management. They have searchable archives that are helpful for finding answers to questions that were asked before you subscribed.

ERIL (Electronic Resources in Libraries)
http://listserv.binghamton.edu/archives/eril-1.html

COLLDV-L
http://serials.infomotions.com/colldv-1

SERIALST
www.uvm.edu/~bmaclenn/serialst.html

ACQNET
http://acqweb.org/acqnet.html

Print and Electronic Journals

Charleston Advisor (subscription, limited free content)
www.charlestonco.com

NewJour
http://gulib.georgetown.edu/newjour

Against the Grain (subscription, limited free content)
www.against-the-grain.com

Library Journal (subscription, limited free content)
www.libraryjournal.com

ALCTS Newsletter Online
www.ala.org/ala/mgrps/divs/alcts/resources/ano

LIBRES Research Electronic Journal
http://libres.curtin.edu.au

Directories

EBSCO: Serials Directory (subscription, may request a free trial)
www.ebscohost.com/academic/the-serials-directory

Serials Solutions: Ulrich's Periodical Directory (subscription)
www.serialssolutions.com/management/ulrichs

This is also available in print from Bowker
www.bowker.com/index/php/component/content/article/2/487

Unfortunately, there are no free serial directories. While it is possible to use OCLC's WorldCat (www.worldcat.org) for this purpose, it is very cumbersome and not recommended.

EVALUATION OF E-RESOURCES

After selecting prospective e-resources, it is necessary to evaluate each one in order to determine what it will add to the collection. Be sure to ask the vendor for a free trial when evaluating resources. Without a trial it will almost be impossible to determine if a given resource is suitable for your users. The good news is that free trials are a standard offering from vendors because their goal is to increase the number of subscribers. If you plan on allowing users to trial the resource, ask the vendor if there is usage data available after the trial. This data will assist with selection. In addition, initiating a free trial will enable you to evaluate a given resource according to the following criteria:

Content: Review the electronic content. Is the content complete? Are there any similar resources in print? If so, how does the content compare? Is the content accurate?

Users: Is the e-resource of value to your users? What is the usage of print and electronic resources with similar content or in the same subject area?

Interface: Is the interface user-friendly? Does it require complex searching or is there a basic search feature that retrieves relevant search results? Is navigation of the resource intuitive? Are the navigation links and buttons clearly labeled? Is it easy to clear results and begin a new search? Is the allotment of time before the resource times out (when the search session ceases) generous? Are there help screens and/or tutorials for users?

Currency: What is the date coverage of the material? Is the date coverage adequate for the subject matter and for your users? How frequently is the resource updated? Does the provider impose embargoes on full-text journals? An embargo is the length of time between an issue's initial publication and full-text availability in the resource. Many embargoes are anywhere from six to twenty-four months.

Output: What are the output options such as printing, saving, or e-mailing the document? Are any of the downloading options easy to use? Is the full text in HTML web pages or in PDF? If the output is in PDF can the library assist patrons who are having problems downloading these files remotely?

Access: Is the resource accessed via the Internet, or must it be installed on a computer network? Can the resource be accessed remotely? If so, can it be remotely accessed via proxy server, password, and/or virtual private network (VPN)? What are the bandwidth requirements and are they adequate to accommodate those still using phone landlines to connect to the Internet? Which browsers and what version should be used in order for the resource to function optimally?

Vendor: Investigate the reputation of the vendor. Find reviews of the resource as well as other products from the vendor. Use your network of contacts to find out if other librarians are satisfied with not only the performance of the product, but also with the vendor's customer support.

Usage data: Does the vendor offer meaningful usage data? If so, how are statistics obtained? Are they delivered via e-mail from the vendor, or is it necessary to log into the administrative portal in order to retrieve them? Are they offered in a readable file format such as XLSX (Excel) or CSV (Comma Delimited)?

Cost: Request information on price increases from the vendor and carefully evaluate it within the context of your library's budget. Are the resources reasonably affordable? Are there any pricing plans specifically tailored for smaller libraries? Is the subscription rate negotiable?

License: First, ask the vendor if the resource requires a signed license agreement. Review the license and note restrictions and terms that need to be negotiated. Is the overall license agreement too restrictive or does it require only a few modifications? The next chapter covers the fundamentals of license agreements, but the contract is a major factor in selection. Specifically, if a vendor will not agree to modify the contract, the library may not be able to subscribe to the resource. Conversely, a license agreement may initially have several restrictive terms and the vendor might surprisingly agree to modify them without question upon negotiation.

The aforementioned selection criteria can also be used to create an e-resource selection checklist. Here are some examples:

Library of Congress
www.loc.gov/catdir/bibcontrol/selection_criteria.pdf

American Library Association
www.ala.org/rusa/resources/guidelines/guidelinesintroduction

University of Maryland
www.lib.umd.edu/CLMD/COLL.Policies/elecrescdp.html

United States Department of Agriculture, National Agricultural Library
www.nal.usda.gov/about/policy/coll_dev_add2.shtml

Baylor University
www.baylor.edu/lib/electrres/index.php?id=31954

Law Librarians of Puget Sound (LLOPS)
http://llops.org/?s=electronic+resource&x=0&y=0

University of North Dakota
http://webapp.und.edu/dept/library/Departments/abc/echklst1.htm

WHAT ABOUT OPEN-ACCESS E-RESOURCES?

Thus far, we have focused on e-resource subscriptions. As a small library with a modest budget, it is essential to consider adding open-access e-resources to your collection. Open-access electronic publications are often scholarly resources that allow unrestricted access and have no subscription costs. An increasing number of open-access publications are e-books and e-book chapters. It is important to understand that some e-resources offer only part of their content as Open Access. For example, many journal publishers offer back files or archived content as open access, but current content is accessed only with a paid subscription. The beauty or frustration of open access (depending on how you look at it) is that while many electronic publications are migrating to this mode of delivery, there are also open-access publications that cease to exist. Keeping up with these changes is very challenging and requires vigilance in tracking open access resources.

There are several key resources that will serve as a guide to understanding more about open-access initiatives as well as open-access title lists for e-resource collection development. Before you delve into selection, please read Peter Suber's "A Very Brief Introduction to Open Access" (www.earlham.edu/~peters/fos/brief.htm). Also, review SPARC's (Scholarly Publishing and Resources Coalition) website (www.arl.org/sparc/publications/index.shtml). SPARC's primary interest is in exploring new models of scholarly communication, and they are one of the forerunners in the open-access publication movement. Some readers may find the Open Access Directory (http://oad.simmons.edu/oadwiki/Main_Page) more useful because it assumes visitors do not have any prior knowledge of the subject.

Directories of Open Access e-Resources

There are many resources that can assist you with finding open-access journals, e-books, and e-book chapters. This is certainly not an exhaustive list—there are many more open-access resources available and the number grows exponentially with each year.

DOAJ (Directory of Open Access Journals)
www.doaj.org

Open J-Gate
www.openj-gate.com/Search/QuickSearch.aspx

BioMed Central
www.biomedcentral.com/info/libraries/oajournals

Open Access Journals Search Engine
http://oajse.com

PLOS (Public Library of Science)
www.plos.org/publications/journals

PKP (Public Knowledge Project)
http://pkp.sfu.ca/ojs-journals

Open Science Directory
www.opensciencedirectory.net

The Open Library
    http://openlibrary.org (e-books)

Bartleby—Great Books Online
    www.bartleby.com

World eBook Library
    http://netlibrary.net/WorldHome.html

THE KNOWLEDGE BASE AND A–Z ELECTRONIC JOURNAL LIST

Originally intended to provide a central point for electronic journal collections, the knowledge base has evolved to become a comprehensive database that contains metadata, not only for electronic journals, but also for print journals, Open-access journal titles, electronic state and federal depository documents, and even electronic books. Simply put, it is a database of the library's holdings. Many vendors, such as EBSCO, TDNet, Ex Libris, and Serials Solutions, offer knowledge base support and development for an annual paid subscription. CUFTS, developed by Simon Frasier University, is an open-source knowledge base that also has paid hosted options for a nominal fee. Vendor-based knowledge bases and CUFTS— even though it is open source and implies local installation—work with publishers and providers to make sure the knowledge base is as accurate as possible. It is then the responsibility of the subscriber (library) to activate each resource to convey local holdings. Furthermore, the library may customize it to include or exclude any of the library's resources. For example, some libraries opt to exclude print journals from the knowledge base.

One of the most critical functions of the knowledge base is to serve as a back-end database that provides content for the publicly accessible A–Z journal list. Despite the growing trend of including all types of materials in the knowledge base, the A–Z list is still commonly referred to as the electronic journal A–Z list. For the purpose of the discussion of A–Z lists, we will refer to them as A–Z journal lists. Usually these front-end interfaces are locally named Journal Locator, Journal Finder, Locate Journals, etc. In addition, the front-end interfaces are customizable with a few website programming languages (mostly XHTML and CSS) in order for the interface to incorporate local branding.

Knowledge base management is essential for accurately reflecting the library's holdings. It is also a key element in linking citation to full-text articles. The OpenURL protocol allows citation to full-text articles.

Access to More Content with Help from the Knowledge Base: OpenURL Link Resolvers

Many libraries still have abstract and index (A&I) databases and/or databases that only have partial full-text content. What if the citation and abstract are available in a different database in your library's collection? How would you be able to quickly discover this? OpenURL link resolvers accomplish this feat in a matter of seconds. OpenURL is a NISO standard (Z39.88) which allows the creation of web links (URLs) that contain metadata enabling the direct linking to full-text articles, books, etc. Once the link resolver interprets and accepts the metadata of the OpenURL, the link resolver searches the library's knowledge base. When there is a match, the link resolver determines if there is an item-level link that is based on locally administered rules (for example, some libraries will exclude linking to abstracts) that takes the user to the full-text article from a different resource. The availability of full-text articles will display in a user-interface menu. Then, the user can click on the link and view the full-text article. If there is no match, many OpenURL link resolvers offer a menu that includes a link to interlibrary loan services.

As one can imagine, many libraries are heavily reliant on OpenURL technology and subscribe to OpenURL link resolvers. There are a few open-source link resolvers, but many of them require advanced technical skills. Here is a list of resources where you can find out more about OpenURL link resolvers:

Library of Congress OpenURL Products and Vendors
www.loc.gov/catdir/lcpaig/openurl.html

Tennant, Roy. "OpenURL"
http://techessence.info/openurl

Apps, Ann and Ross MacIntyre. "Why OpenURL?"
www.dlib.org/dlib/may06/apps/05apps.html

oss4Lib (Open Source for Libraries) OpenURL
www.oss4lib.org/taxonomy/term/82

ELECTRONIC RESOURCE MANAGEMENT SYSTEMS (ERMS)

Developing e-resource collections poses many unique challenges, but so does managing them. In fact, librarians have struggled for years with how to efficiently manage e-resources as they move through the life cycle—from a trial subscription to the decision to discontinue a subscription. All of these processes require communication and administrative savvy, and librarians were becoming increasingly frustrated with paper trails, e-mail folder systems, and the like. Librarians also needed a database to store license agreements, vendor contact information, and usage statistics. Even though small libraries have fewer e-resources, they still need to effectively manage their resources.

Electronic resource management systems (ERMS) were developed in response to this universal need among libraries, and they garnered a lot of attention during the early 2000s. These systems were designed primarily to manage e-resource workflows; provide storage for license agreements; upload usage data—either automatically using the SUSHI protocol or manually—store administrative information such as usernames and passwords, vendor contact information, holdings, and coverage data; assist with fund management and financial reporting; etc. Although there has been some discussion regarding the efficacy of current electronic resource management systems in managing workflows, the systems have been extremely useful for storing license agreement data and vendor contact information. Some libraries employ their ERM database records to serve as the public interface of their database of databases.

Many vendor-based ERMSs are rather expensive for the small library, costing upwards of $20,000, not including annual maintenance fees. If cost is not an impediment to subscribing to a commercial ERMS, then it is a very simple matter to investigate them. Publications such as *Against the Grain* and *Library Journal* often cover them in great detail. What should be covered here are the outstanding free and low-cost options that are suitable for a small library.

> E-Matrix (www.lib.ncsu.edu/e-matrix)
> > Developed at North Carolina State University, E-Matrix is an open-source electronic resource management system that is currently not available to the public, but it is under development in order to offer it to other libraries worldwide.

CORAL (http://erm.library.nd.edu)

ERMes (http://murphylibrary.uwlax.edu/erm)

Trueserials (http://trueserials.com)

Gold Rush (www.coalliance.org/grinfo)
    Developed by the Colorado Alliance of Research Libraries.

CONCLUSION

Despite limited budgets, smaller libraries must be poised to respond to the electronic resources revolution within the constraints of their unique situations. Migrating from print, where it makes sense, will provide several advantages for your library and for your patrons. Carefully selected, e-resources will greatly enhance content access for your patrons, providing them with faster and remote access and much greater usability. E-resources paired with knowledge base management systems and OpenURL link resolvers will augment your ability to track usage and provision your resources most effectively to meet your patrons' needs. This will also assist with ensuring that content you provide is located by the patrons who need it. In the following chapter, we will explore the basics of license agreements, which are the method by which libraries acquire e-resources and provide the rules that govern their permitted use.

SUGGESTED READINGS

Gregory, Vicki L. 2006. *Selecting and Managing Electronic Resources: A How-To-Do-It Manual for Librarians.* New York: Neal-Schuman.

Kovacs, Diane K. and Kara L. Robinson. 2004. *The Kovacs Guide to Electronic Library Collection Development: Essential Core Subject Collections, Selection Criteria, and Guidelines.* New York: Neal-Schuman.

TERMS: Techniques for Electronic Resources Management. http://library.hud.ac.uk/wikiterms/Main_Page.

The E-Resources Management Handbook. http://uksg.metapress.com/content/120087.

Licensing Electronic Resources

Rachel A. Erb

In the last chapter we discussed e-resources and the advantages they offer for your library. The rules governing the acquisition of e-resources are different from those for print resources. Unlike print resources, which are owned by the library, e-resources are generally licensed for a period of time (including perpetually) and carry specific rules regarding their legal usage. Thus, someone at the library must be familiar with the basics of handling license agreements.

During the print-dominant era of library materials, libraries purchased all their content in the form of physical items. In the modern era, libraries are purchasing both print and electronic resources. Unlike print materials, which the library owns, electronic resources, in general, are only leased from a general aggregator or vendor such as ProQuest or EBSCO. What this means is that traditional ownership of materials is gradually being supplanted by contracts that must be renewed over a given term established by the content provider. In some cases, however, the license is perpetual, meaning that as long as the terms are adhered to by both parties, the content is owned indefinitely by the library. Thus, license agreements are necessary. Simply stated, a license agreement is a legal contract between two parties, the licensor and the licensee (http://us legal.com). The legal contract, according to FindLaw.com's legal dictionary, is "an agreement between two or more parties that creates in each party a duty to do or not to do something and a right to performance of the other's duty or remedy for the breach of the other's duty" (http://dictionary.findlaw.com/definition/contract.html). Because a license agreement is a contract, the terms *license* and *contract* will be used interchangeably throughout this chapter.

License agreements are an integral part of the subscription to aggregator databases, electronic journals and books, computer software, streaming films, web content, financial resources, and even user- or institution-generated content such as locally digitized collections. Even small or solo-operated libraries that do not purchase any electronic resources should be concerned with license agreements because, in many cases, these libraries rely on statewide initiatives that provide databases gratis. These statewide purchases are based on license agreements whose terms must be adhered to even if the participating library has not contributed any subscription costs.

Publishers and providers of electronic content draft license agreements as a means to control use and access. Some license agreements may contain clauses that directly conflict with the needs of the library because they are too restrictive and include unreasonable terms that will sometimes even discount legal rights. Therefore, someone in the library organization needs to understand license agreements and be able to effectively negotiate terms to ensure the library is benefitting from the contract.

While it is impossible to cover all aspects of licensing in the electronic environment in one chapter, the aim here is to present a brief, clear overview of licensing for those with no familiarity with the topic. This introduction serves as a foundation for the reader to be able to explore more detailed sources.

APPROACHING LICENSING AGREEMENTS: LOOK BEFORE YOU LEAP

It is tempting to rush into signing license agreements so the library can subscribe to the content and offer the service to their patrons in a timely manner. Signing off on an agreement without the library reviewing the document beforehand is not advisable. Optimally, the contract should be a mutually beneficial agreement—a document that reflects equally both parties' rights. Prior to initiating the subscription process, the library should have a list of what the agreement should include in order for the library to sign the contract.

The following checklist is based on Lesley Ellen Harris's recommendations in her book *Licensing Digital Content: A Practical Guide for Librarians*. Before even reviewing a licensing agreement, ask yourself the following questions (the license elements in bold are essential):

> **Content:** What kind of content is the library interested in licensing? E-books? Aggregators? Electronic journals?

Site definition: Will a single library be covered under this agreement or multiple branches or campuses?

Authorized user definition: How will the library define "authorized users"? Faculty, staff, and students? Walk-in users? Local researchers?

User rights: What rights should your users have? Printing? Downloading?

Remote access/authentication: How will the library authenticate authorized users? Will the library provide remote access via proxy server?

Interlibrary loan/course packs/reserves: How does the library plan to use the content besides making it available for their patron base? Interlibrary loan? Course packs? Reserves?

Interlibrary loan: If interested in offering electronic content via interlibrary loan, does the library have a delivery method that is preferable? Automated document delivery via e-mail? Print and mail via postal service?

Governing body of law and jurisdiction: What state or province laws should govern the license? If the library is a state-funded entity, what are the laws regarding jurisdiction? Can your library accept a legal venue outside of the state, province, or country in which the library is located? Alternatively, is it acceptable for the content provider to remain silent on the legal venue? (Remaining silent means the legal venue is not stated in the contract.)

Indemnifications: What is your institution's policy regarding indemnification? Does your state have an anti-indemnity statute?

Breach/remedy or cure: If there is a material breach, does the library have the resources to cure the breach within the allotted time stipulated by the contract? What would be the minimum amount of time that would be reasonable for the library to cure the breach?

Outage/System Downtime Notifications: It should be imperative that the content provider notify the library of downtime and maintenance. What is the preferred method of notification and how much notification is adequate?

Warranties: Will the library require the vendor to agree to specific performance warranties? If these warranties are not met, is it imperative that the library receive recompense in some form?

Confidentiality: Is the library comfortable with the vendor's demands for confidentiality of the agreement and/or subscription rate for the library? Conversely, will the library require the vendor to respect the confidentiality of patron data?

Content Changes: How does the library prefer to be notified when content is either removed or added to the resource? Can the library accept that many providers do not provide any notification and the onus is on the subscriber to investigate changes?

Perpetual access: Would the library prefer to have access to content covered under the subscription period in the event the resource is cancelled?

Subscription period: How often would the library prefer for the license to renew? Annually? Biannually? Every three years? Would the library prefer that the product renew automatically after a given interval?

Additional Questions to Consider

Are there any required provisions the library must include?

Who will be responsible for handling negotiations?

Who will be available to assist with more complex legal issues? Is there a consulting attorney available?

Who will sign the final agreement?

LICENSE AGREEMENTS: BASIC STRUCTURE

Once all questions are answered and a library's terms are composed, it is time to examine several sample license agreements. Start by going to the generic license agreement posted by Liblicense (www.library.yale.edu/~llicense/standlicagree.1st .html). This exercise will help you become familiar with the language and terms of license agreements. Keep in mind sample agreements reflect the ideal coverage and depth of a contract. Actual vendor contracts may fall short of this standard—prior to negotiation, of course! Since that is often the case, these sample contracts help the licensee frame negotiations that will enable the library to have the same rights as the vendor.

While each license agreement varies in content, the following is a checklist of some common license elements that will assist you when reviewing license agreements:

Definitions: This part of the agreement lists terms defined by the vendor. For example, vendors will often differ in what constitutes a single-site, authorized users, etc. Read this section carefully before reviewing the rest of the agreement.

Grant of license: This section officially states the licensor grant the licensee nonexclusive access of the resource. There may also be a subsection indicating the nature of materials subject to the agreement.

Fees and payment: The licensor discloses pricing models, payment terms, and renewals.

Site definition: Libraries that have several branches may not have all locations covered in the agreement. This section of the license specifies covered physical locations.

Authorized users: This defines the library's patron base that is permitted to use the licensed resource: faculty, staff, students, walk-in users, etc.

Authorized uses: This section enumerates how the licensed resource can be accessed or used for various purposes such as interlibrary loan, scholarly sharing, reserves, course packs, etc.

Interlibrary loan: Sometimes this is a separate section or a distinct subsection of Authorized Uses. Interlibrary loan permissions and arrangements are discussed.

Archival rights: This right is not always granted in agreements, but it occurs frequently enough to warrant including in the list. The licensor is granting a perpetual license for the licensee to archive content from the resource during the subscription term after the subscription is cancelled.

Confidentiality: A statement of mutual agreement between the licensor and licensee to maintain user confidentiality of any usage data, including usernames and passwords. The licensor will sometimes specify that the licensee must not share the contents of the agreement and/or the subscription fees with other subscribers. This, of course, is not reasonable and should be modified.

Breach remedy/cure: User behavior (i.e., excessive downloading) often results in a breach of contract. The licensor will state how the breach is communicated and how much time is allotted for the licensee to cure the breach before access is suspended.

Force majeure: Neither licensor nor licensee will be liable for any damages or have the right to terminate the agreement if caused by circumstances beyond its control such as acts of nature, government restrictions, wars, etc.

Warranties: In this section (usually printed in all capital letters), the licensor makes no warranties regarding errors, quality, or harm caused by a computer virus, etc. The licensor will usually state that the licensed materials are provided on an "as-is" basis. Ideally, this section will also include a clause that neither party will be liable for any indirect or inconsequential damages.

Indemnification: Both the licensor and licensee (sometimes stated as mutual indemnity) agree to indemnify and hold the other party harmless against claims, losses, or damages.

Governing law: The agreement will be interpreted according to laws of a particular state, county, province, or country.

Notice: This brief section indicates how notices are communicated to the licensor.

Signatures: At the end of the agreement there is a section for authorized signatures.

OTHER TYPES OF LICENSE AGREEMENTS: CLICK-THROUGH, PASSIVE TERMS, AND CREATIVE COMMONS

Click-through agreements are contractual agreements that a user views online and accepts the terms of by clicking on a box or button indicating assent. Passive agreements are contracts that are enforced despite the fact that these agreements either require one signature, often the licensee's, or none at all. Passive agreements are often frustratingly buried within the publisher's website, but in the case of electronic journals, the vendor will be able to assist with locating the terms. Click-through agreements or other means of passive assent have been upheld in the courts as fully enforceable. Therefore, even though these agreements are online, do not require signatures, and are often very brief, the library is legally liable for adhering to all the enumerated terms and ensuring that patrons do the same.

There may be some objectionable terms in these agreements that will jeopardize your institution in the case of an infraction. It is, therefore, in the library's best interest to negotiate for modifications such as legal venue. If the publisher agrees, make sure it is documented in writing—either as a PDF, Word document, or e-mail. This document will serve to protect the library against any future allegations of violating the contract.

Creative Commons license agreements allow content creators to communicate the rights they reserve and waive for the benefit of users and other creators. A Creative Commons license allows the content creator to retain copyright and to dictate how the content is to be used. These agreements are brief; they also do not require negotiations and signatures. Open-access electronic journals and electronic resource packages such as the Public Library of Science (www.plos.org) and BioMed Central (www.biomedcentral.com) often license their content via Creative Commons. Again, these are license agreements, so the library is legally liable for any violations. There is no need to negotiate for the modification of license terms because Creative Commons licenses are less restrictive than even click-through or passive license agreements. The flexibility of terms and responsibilities makes licensing via Creative Commons particularly attractive for nonprofit and educational entities. Awareness of these agreements will serve you well in the future as they continue to rise in popularity among organizations that are content providers for libraries.

LICENSE AGREEMENTS: NEGOTIATIONS

Because many libraries differ in what they can accept in a contract, it would be impossible to give tips for negotiating license agreements that would be applicable to all libraries. The creation of the aforementioned checklist will serve as a guide in negotiating agreements. There are, however, a few problematic terms that one will often encounter in an agreement that no library should accept under any circumstances. If a vendor resists modifying any of these terms, it is advisable to walk away without hesitation.

> **Indemnification.** Never agree to indemnify or hold harmless a provider against damage claims, losses, penalties, or injuries the licensee or authorized users incur which arise from a third-party claim that alleges

contract breach and copyright or intellectual property infringement. If you agree to indemnify a provider, you will be responsible for the damages of any third-party claims.

Jurisdiction. Do not agree that the license will be interpreted according to the laws of a state, province, or country other than where the library exists. Offer a counterproposal that either the venue is in the library's jurisdiction or agree to remain silent on the venue.

There are changes to terms without notification from the vendor. Make sure the license includes terms that state any alterations will be accompanied by notification and a written agreement or addendum. Otherwise, the library will be subject to the whims of the vendor and held liable for any violations regardless of being notified about them prior to the offense.

An unreasonable amount of time to cure a breach. Licenses often state that access to a resource will be terminated immediately upon a material breach by the library. Breaches are common, and it is reasonable to ask for specific amount of time to remedy the breach. Strive for thirty days, but fifteen is acceptable. Fewer than fifteen days could unduly burden a smaller library. It is up to your individual library to decide what works best. The bottom line is never to accept immediate termination upon committing a material breach.

An unreasonable amount of time to pay an invoice. Payments, even for renewals, often require the involvement and subsequent approval of several individuals. In some libraries, authorization for payment resides with a board of directors. Never agree to these terms because it will be nearly impossible to meet this obligation and will result in a temporary loss of access if the invoice is not paid within the restrictive time frame.

Library is legally responsible for user actions. Some license agreements stipulate that the library must make sure the user is responsible for his or her rights regarding use of the product. There are even terms stating the library is responsible for making sure the user understands all the terms while indicating the provider can change them at any time without notice. Never agree to the library being held legally responsible for users under any circumstances. Offer a counterproposal that the library will make a reasonable effort to inform and educate users of appropriate use of the product.

Interlibrary loan is prohibited. Participating in interlibrary loan is an integral part of participating in the national and international community as a whole. Not every library can afford every single resource on the market. Endeavor to negotiate for the right to offer interlibrary loan for articles in the resource. Better yet, include a provision that all interlibrary loans will be in compliance with section 108 of the U.S. Copyright Act. Section 108 mandates that libraries are permitted to participate in interlibrary loan arrangements as long as the copies are not intended to add to a library's collection, and therefore, substitute for a subscription of the resource.

Walk-in users are prohibited. If your library is a funded by the state, province, or county, then this is in conflict with the library's obligations. Never agree to those terms as a publicly funded institution.

ALTERNATIVE LICENSE AGREEMENTS: SHARED ELECTRONIC RESOURCE UNDERSTANDING

Negotiating license agreements is very time consuming, and, therefore, often burdensome. In addition, small publishers and vendors often have difficulties navigating the contract negotiation process; they are hampered by not having access to a contract attorney for assistance with drafting and negotiating detailed license agreements. SERU (Shared E-Resource Understanding) resolves these problems for both licensor and licensee. Specifically, "SERU offers publishers and libraries an opportunity to save both time and the costs associated with a negotiated and signed license agreement by agreeing to operate within a framework of shared understanding and good faith" (www.niso.org/publications/rp/RP-7–2008.pdf).

Shared understanding is key to the concept of SERU as it is not a license agreement. SERU encompasses "common understanding for publishers and libraries" as an alternative to a contract agreement. Because SERU is not a license agreement it is devoid of clauses addressing jurisdiction, indemnification, and warranties. SERU agreements, instead, include terms regarding the subscription itself, authorized users, appropriate and inappropriate use, confidentiality, performance of product, and archiving and perpetual access (www.niso.org/publications/rp/RP-7–2008.pdf).

While SERU has many advantages, many publishers and vendors do not participate in SERU. If you are uncertain if a particular publisher or vendor does participate in SERU, it is best to refer to the SERU registry: www.niso.org/workrooms/seru/

67

registry. Also, keep in mind that just because a publisher or vendor is listed in the registry does not mean that the licensor will automatically enter a SERU agreement for all subscriptions.

SERU agreements are very simple, but sometimes the library may have additional concerns. Special terms the library or vendor/publisher would like to include can be easily incorporated in the agreement as an addendum document or an e-mail. There are times when it is valid to forgo SERU. If the library is not comfortable with the vendor or publisher and has additional, complicated questions regarding terms of use, then it is worth the effort to resort to traditional negotiated and signed contracts.

CONCLUSION

License agreements require close reading and examination. Even though smaller and one-person libraries handle fewer licenses than larger institutions, it is still important for each agreement to be properly interpreted and managed. This chapter offered a brief introduction to licensing materials.

LICENSING ELECTRONIC RESOURCES

Anderson, Rick. 2003. *Buying and Contracting for Resources and Services.* New York: Neal-Schuman.

Harris, Lesley Ellen. 2009. *Licensing Digital Content: A Practical Guide for Librarians,* 2nd ed. Chicago: American Library Association.

International Federation of Library Associations and Institutions. 2001. "Licensing Principles." March. http://archive.ifla.org/V/ebpb/copy.htm.

LibLicense. www.library.yale.edu/~llicense/index.shtml.

Phillips, Kara. 2006. "Deal or No Deal—Licensing and Acquiring Digital Resources: License Negotiations." November. www.llrx.com/columns/dea13.htm.

SERU. 2009. "FAQ on SERU: A Shared Electronic Resource Understanding." July. www.niso.org/workrooms/seru/faq/SERUFAQaug2010.pdf.

University of California Libraries. 2006. "Principles for Acquiring and Licensing Information in Digital Formats." July. http://libraries.universityofcalifornia.edu/cdc/principlesforacquiring.html.

PART 3

The Virtual Library

Web Page Development

Rene J. Erlandson

Like physical libraries, virtual libraries encompass a broad array of collections, resources, and services. Creating a virtual library can seem overwhelming when faced with little technical support or limited time to devote to development. However, just like geo-libraries (traditional brick-and-mortar buildings constrained by physical geographic locations), virtual libraries have common basic components that can be developed over time. The most basic building block of every virtual library is the web page. A web page is a document or location on the World Wide Web that is accessible via a web browser. Multiple web pages linked together as a library website can provide access to a host of library resources, including the library catalog, online databases, virtual collections, and reference assistance. In addition, library websites often function as a platform to announce events happening in the library and provide access to library information such as address, phone numbers, and library hours. While most visitors to library websites enter via a desktop computer, a growing number of virtual library guests use mobile devices to access library web pages. Most desktop sites are unattractive and cumbersome to navigate on mobile devices. Therefore, in addition to creating standard library desktop websites, librarians are creating separate library mobile websites to meet the needs of the growing number of mobile device users, thus adding another component to the virtual library. With a minimal investment of time and effort you can begin to develop a virtual presence for both sets of users.

DESIGNING A LIBRARY DESKTOP WEBSITE

Building a library web page of any kind no longer requires an intimate knowledge of scripting code like HTML (hypertext markup language). Many site generators allow you to visually design a site while the software creates the markup behind the scenes. A basic understanding of markup language can be useful but is by no means essential to creating a functional, attractive, engaging website.

Where to Start?

Although beauty is in the eye of the beholder, usability studies performed on a variety of library websites found the majority of virtual library visitors preferred a streamlined, simple design. Just because scripting allows for blinking text and gyrating images does not mean users wish to be bombarded with these distractions while visiting a library website. Functional library websites allow visitors to quickly access what they are seeking. Visitors should never be more than two or three clicks away from the information they need. The most successful library website combines easy access with attractive design elements.

Before beginning to build your first library web page, take time to visit other library websites. A couple of resources that collate a variety of library websites in one location are Website Design (www.libsuccess.org/index.php?title=Website_Design) and LibWeb (http://worldcat.org/arcviewer/5/OCC/2011/08/30/H1314729484639/viewer/file1.html). While browsing within a site, critique the functionality and design of the site. Is it easy to navigate within the site? Is the site attractive? Are the terms used within the site descriptive of the information contained within corresponding links or information? Think of yourself as a library visitor and perform a common task on each site—locate a specific journal, find out about wireless access, etc. Were you able to locate the information? Was the information difficult or easy to find? By visiting other library websites, you will begin to understand how design affects functionality.

Defining specific desired goals for a website assists in developing an implementation plan. So, begin the website development process by defining the desired end product. What is the ultimate goal of the site? Will the site provide access to library resources? Serve as a clearinghouse for library information? Act as a promotional tool? Function as a gathering place for library related activities? Or will the site serve all of the aforementioned purposes? Every aspect of a website does not need to be developed at one time. However, a full analysis of final expected outcomes for the library website will result in a cohesive approach to the design of each web page within the site and ultimately provide a better user experience for website visitors. We have all visited sites that seem unorganized, confusing, and counterintuitive to use. Odds are these sites were designed without a plan.

Once you have delineated your ultimate goals, it is time to identify the components needed to reach them. If a desired goal is to enable visitors to search the library catalog, a catalog search box will need to be included within the site. If you want to create a space where teen readers can share thoughts and information with one another, the website will need to include a collaborative author space where it is possible for community members to post thoughts, questions, and responses. Also, consider what content needs to be on the home page (first or initial page of a website) and what content can be located on other pages within the site. At this point, it may be helpful to create a diagram of content for each web page, also known as a site map. As you determine website goals and the components needed to accomplish the goals, also consider the terminology to be used within the website and include these terms on your site map. Stay away from library jargon, such as *circulation*, *interlibrary loan*, and *reference*. Make sure common language is used within the website, such as *check out*, *borrow material from another library*, or *ask a question*. It is important to remember that library websites are created for people outside of the library.

Once the components and corresponding terminology are decided upon, decide on the location of every component within the website. Keep in mind the graphic design principle of proximity—like information, images, etc., should be placed together within a design. Identify information and links to be included on the home page and each subsequent page. A general rule of thumb is to include fewer than forty links on any given page, if possible. More than forty links on a page can end up looking cluttered and make it difficult for visitors to identify where the information they seek can be found. Including white space (open or blank space) in a design creates the streamlined environment most website visitors prefer. White space should be used to delineate information or categories of information within a page. White space provides an area for the eye to rest within a site and helps visitors locate what they seek on the page.

Content Best Practices

Use common language, not library jargon.

Group like information together within web pages.

Include fewer than forty links on any page.

Information should be no more than three clicks away from the home page.

How to Create an Engaging Online Environment

Developers often rush through (or skip) defining the goals and content of a site, in favor of creating the aesthetic of a website, in part because visitors immediately notice the look of a website and react to it. If a website is unattractive visitors will leave the site with a less-than-favorable impression of the virtual library, even if they find the information they need within the site. However, although visitors are generally unaware of the underlying structure and content of a website, until they cannot find what they are looking for within the site, these aspects of design are as important as aesthetic. The content and structure of a website directly affect ease of navigation and access within a site. Successful websites contain what visitors seek and are structured to allow quick access to that information. While the design aesthetic determines visitors' first impressions of the virtual library, appropriate content that is quickly navigable will keep visitors coming back. Therefore, it is important to create a website that is functional as well as attractive.

Following standard graphic design principles—contrast, repetition, alignment, and proximity—will help you create an attractive, engaging virtual library environment. Color is the primary design element of any website. Therefore, it is important to understand the basic principles of color theory as the foundation for a visually attractive website. Tiger Color (www.tigercolor.com/color-lab/color-theory/color-theory-intro.htm) provides a brief introduction to color theory, explaining the significance of and response to various color schemes. Analogous color schemes (colors next to each other on the color wheel) mimic the color schemes found in nature. Analogous color schemes are considered harmonious and pleasing to the eye, while contrasting colors (colors opposite each other on the color wheel) create the most impact. Although the use of intense contrasting colors as site background colors is not recommended, contrasting colors can be used to draw the eye to a designated area within a web page. Contrast creates impact. When selecting colors to be used in a website, select background colors, text colors, and image colors within an overall scheme.

At times colors for a website may be dictated by institution or local community colors (the college colors are orange and blue or the local high school colors are red and green, for example). If you were to use orange and blue as the background colors for an entire website, it would be overwhelming for visitors. Instead, mitigate the vibrancy of contrasting color combinations by using them in small amounts within the site, or choosing lighter shades of the primary colors (light blue and peach). When selecting background colors for websites remember text will be displayed on the colors and will need to be readable. Keep in mind, results of website usability studies indicate participants found dark text on light background easy to read, while white text on dark backgrounds is the most difficult combination to read (and may not be compliant with Section 508 of the US Rehabilitation Act). At the end of the day, web page design is about readability. Therefore, choose a color scheme that is easily readable in all levels of light, on all screen sizes.

Once a color scheme is chosen, carry it through to every page within the website. Repetitive use of colors, logos, and images between elements of a virtual library creates a library brand (or look). Also, use one font throughout the website to facilitate readability and create a consistent appearance, varying the size and strength of the font for emphasis and detail. Repetition of design elements like color and font throughout a website creates a cohesive environment for visitors. Changing colors and fonts from one web page to another within a site can create a feeling of chaos and uncertainty for visitors.

An image may be worth a thousand words, but the converse is not true. A designer must be careful not only to keep text on pages to a minimum, but also to limit the use of images and graphics within a web page. Adding dancing books, flashing text, and other superfluous imagery will make pages more difficult to read and slower to load. When using multiple images to replace words, make sure meaning is implicit for everyone, and use repetitive elements like size to create unity within the form. It is important to find a balance between text, imagery, and white space within a web page design.

Design Best Practices

Simple is better, less is more.

Group like information together within web pages.

Nothing should be placed on the page arbitrarily.

Analogous color schemes are the most harmonious.

Contrasting colors draw the eye to designated areas or text.

Dark text on a light background is easiest to read.

Use repetitive elements (like color and font) throughout a site to create a cohesive virtual environment, or library brand.

Web pages should be readable in most light levels and on most screens.

Web pages should comply with Section 508 of the US Rehabilitation Act.

The underlying structure of displayed data on a web page is referred to as the layout of the page. Most site generators allow designers to select from a number of layout templates, including header, footer, multiple columns, and horizontal or vertical navigation bars. When choosing a web page layout, it is important to consider how information will be aligned within each of the template options. Remember the graphic design rule of proximity—like information and images should be placed together within a design. As the size of information groups and other graphic elements are considered, a layout may become obvious. Be careful not to crowd entries on a web page; make sure to leave enough space between links and information so that visitors can navigate through the site with ease.

The Johnson County Library home page, shown in figure 7.1, follows accepted website design standards.

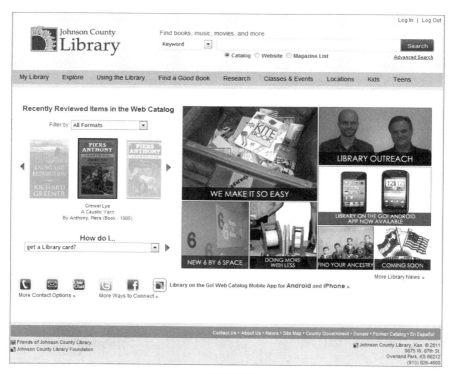

FIGURE 7.1
Example of site that follows graphic design
and website design standards

Free and Low-Cost Platforms

One of the most comprehensive free website generators available to developers is provided by the Internet giant Google. Google Sites (www.google.com/sites) allows web developers to create web pages from scratch, or customize one of the dozens of templates found within the system to quickly design a professional looking web page or site. Google Sites provides developers with 100MB of space, allowing for construction of multiple pages to form a complete website, hosted by Google. No advertising is added to pages created through the service, so visitors will not be bombarded with pop-ups or sidebars filled with ads. Google Sites allows developers to tailor every aspect of system created pages. Developers may create customized URLs for web pages to facilitate easy access. It is also possible to create unique sites even when using templates found within the service by editing the site appearance, layout, colors, and fonts within More Actions or Manage Site. So, if a developer likes the layout of the public library template available in the site template catalog under Schools & Education but doesn't like the colors, it is possible to customize the template by changing the color scheme. In addition, by incorporating customizable Google Gadgets from the Gadget Gallery for current weather, news, RSS feeds etc., a novice developer is able to include dynamic content on web pages. Another positive feature of websites created with Google Sites is they are crawled (indexed) and available via the Google search engine within a week, whereas it may take months for sites created outside the Google environment to be crawled and available through the Google search engine.

One unique feature of Google Sites is the ability to incorporate collaborative authoring into the development of a web page or site. Developers may set up parameters for a web page, or areas within a web page, allowing individuals or groups to edit or add content within the page. So, if a library wants to host an online community events calendar on the library website and allow specific individuals or groups within the community to post directly to the calendar, it is possible on a web page created via Google Sites.

A couple of low-cost, easy-to-use website generators are Yola and Intuit. Pricing for Yola (www.yola.com) begins at $4.95 per month. After creating an account, the system guides a developer through a series of questions and answers used to generate a website. The system even suggests linking pages based on the Website Category a developer chooses. Designers are able to modify color schemes and upload images within the templates. The system does not allow collaborative authoring within published pages, so if collaboration is a desired website feature,

77

this product may not be suitable. Yola has a variety of templates associated with each price level and there is an additional charge for custom domains.

Intuit (www.intuit.com/website-building-software) allows developers to try out the system for thirty days free before purchasing it. After the trial period, subscription rates begin at $7.99 per month. Intuit provides hosting services as well as custom domain names to subscribers. Developers may choose from over 2,000 design templates, or create a custom design.

Website Usage Assessment

Once you create a website it is important to maintain the site. Are people finding the site and, if so, how are they locating it? Which areas of the site receive the most (or least) hits? How do visitors navigate within the site? Identifying how a site is used, and then modifying the site based on that use, will assist you in keeping the site relevant and engaging to community members over time. The most widely used website analysis tool is free. Google Analytics (www.google.com/analytics) supplies web analytics for any website. After signing up for a free Google Analytics account, developers identify the website they wish to track. The system generates a script that, once inserted into a website, allows Google Analytics to track all incoming traffic to and movement within a site. If the website being tracked was created with Google Sites, there is no need to paste script into the site. Simply save and finish the Google Analytics account creation, copy the system-generated Google Analytics account number (like UA-XXXXXXX-X), open Google Sites, enable Google Analytics for the site to be tracked (More Actions, Manage Site, General), and paste the Google Analytics account number into the Analytics Web Property ID field. The system automatically begins tracking the site.

Analytics Best Practices

Do not use your personal Gmail account to setup library Google Analytics accounts.

Create a Gmail account for the library to setup Google Analytics.

If you develop more than one library-related website, create a separate Google Analytics account for each website you wish to track.

DEVELOPING A LIBRARY MOBILE WEBSITE

Do You Need a Mobile Website?

In the past, developing a virtual presence for a library focused on desktop computer users. However, the ubiquitous nature of cellphones in our culture and the increase in smartphone sales and accompanying data packages in markets across the country indicates a growing trend for community members to access information via mobile devices. When exploring the possibility of implementing a mobile library initiative it is important to determine if the community will use mobile library services. One way to identify community interest in accessing library information and resources via mobile devices is to examine incoming traffic to the library desktop site and see how much, if any, originates from mobile devices. Free services like Google Analytics can be used to track mobile device traffic to desktop sites. In addition, the service compiles data on specific mobile devices and device platforms used to access a site and the mobile carriers by which visits originated.

Most library websites created for desktop use are not easily viewed and navigable on mobile devices. To see how a desktop site will look on a mobile device, paste the desktop site URL into a mobile optimizer like Google Mobile Site Viewer (www.google.com/gwt/n). The system automatically optimizes the site for mobile device use by stripping out images, gadgets, colors and other formatting. Although mobile site optimizing reformats desktop sites for mobile viewing, the end results are often still cumbersome to navigate.

What Belongs on a Mobile Website?

Before developing a library mobile site it is useful to take a look at sites created by other libraries. M-Libraries (www.libsuccess.org/index.php?title=M-Libraries) is a dynamic wiki list of known U.S. library mobile websites. It is best to visit these sites on various mobile devices to get an idea how the display differs from one mobile device to another. By visiting other library mobile websites, novice developers can begin to see what works and what doesn't work within the mobile environment.

When creating a library mobile site consider how and where the site will be used. Most mobile users are looking for quick information, on the go (often outside). Therefore, the content and design aesthetic of library mobile websites should reflect the way they will be used. Consider content commonly sought by library mobile users: library hours, directions to the library, library phone number, and access to mobile library resources like the online catalog or electronic journals and books. Once you identify information and resources to include on a library mobile website, it is time to think about the site aesthetics.

Mobile Device Design Aesthetics

When choosing colors and font for a library mobile site, remember mobile devices are often used outside in sunlight. Therefore, sites with contrasting background and font colors will be more easily viewable on mobile devices, like dark fonts on light backgrounds. Light colored fonts are difficult to read in sunlight, so they should be avoided in mobile website design. If the colors and font used for the library desktop site are viable options for the mobile site, use them. By repeating the color scheme and fonts used in the original desktop site, a cohesive appearance is created for each aspect of the virtual library, thus branding each component for the institution. If your initial color scheme is not suitable for mobile device viewing, experiment with related colors.

When considering the layout of a mobile device, remember that the site will most often be viewed on a small screen. Visitors will most likely choose options from the site by touching the screen. Therefore, leave adequate space between menu options to facilitate selection by fingertips, rather than a cursor or stylus. A single-column layout for the mobile website is best suited to sites with primarily text content. Limit the number of content lines to less than seven when adding information and links to the single-column layout, so users do not need to scroll down to locate information. However, if an app-like appearance is desired, select a multicolumn layout. Due to the variation in screen sizes for optimal viewing on most screen types limit yourself to less than seven menu options within the app style also.

Figure 7.2 shows a single-column mobile website layout from Florida International University Libraries Mobile. Figure 7.3 shows an app-like mobile website layout from University of California San Diego Libraries Mobile.

Mobile Website Best Practices

Create a separate library mobile website.

Mobile websites are most often used on the go.

Mobile websites are often used outside in sunlight.

Choose single-column layout.

Keep links/content lines to less than seven.

FIGURE 7.2
Florida International University
Libraries Mobile—Example
of single column mobile
website layout

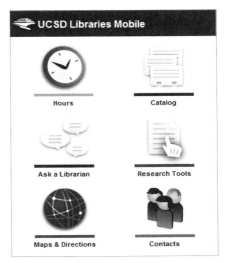

FIGURE 7.3
University of California San
Diego Libraries Mobile—
Example of app-like mobile
website layout

FREE AND LOW-COST PLATFORMS

It is possible to create a mobile site in less than ten minutes using Google Sites (http://sites.google.com). Although the system automatically formats any Google Sites website for viewing on mobile devices, it is important to create a separate website for mobile users because their needs are different. Log in to Google Sites and create a new website, using the same template used for the desktop website created earlier. After naming the page and selecting the template, simplify the layout to one column and save. Next change the site layout, if necessary, and add content.

mobiSiteGalore (www.mobisitegalore.com) is a low-cost mobile website development service. The system does not require developers to have technical expertise. Mobile websites are generated by the system based on selections and data input by the developer. mobiSiteGalore offers a free option to develop up to three pages (without hosting) with paid subscriptions beginning at $49 per year that include hosting.

Although not only a mobile website creator service, LibGuides (www.springshare .com/libguides) is a relatively low-cost hosted content management system that automatically generates mobile formatted pages when system created web pages are accessed via mobile devices. So, in addition to generating mobile web pages, Lib-Guides can be used to create a library desktop site and manage a variety of online content. LibGuides offers a free trial to test out the system. Pricing of LibGuides is calculated after institution information and data are added to a quote request form.

QR CODES

Another mobile device tool many libraries are using is Quick Response (QR) code. A QR code is a barcode readable by mobile devices. When scanned by a mobile device loaded with a QR code reader, visitors are linked directly to information, websites, images, and much more embedded into the codes. Practical applications for QR codes in libraries include linking community members to library hours, way-finding (directions), library contact information, events, exhibits, and much more. Google provides developers with the free QR code generator ZXing (http://zxing.appspot.com/generator) (Zebra Crossing). Using ZXing, it is possible to generate a QR code containing contact information, a calendar event, a phone number, a URL, or actual text in less than a minute by filling in the appropriate information in the code generator template. It is also possible to quickly generate a QR code from a shortened URL created in Google's URL shortener (http://goo.gl) by simply adding .qr after the shortened URL within any browser. Bitly (https://bitly.com) also generates QR codes for URLs shortened within the service. QR codes are an easy way for libraries to test local interest in mobile access of library information and resources. The codes can easily be included in print and online advertisements or printed off and posted throughout the library and city.

CONCLUSION

Virtual libraries are becoming as commonplace on the digital landscape as the physical libraries developed in the twentieth century. Over 1.2 billion personal computers are owned worldwide (Wolfram Research 2011) indicating technology is an integral part of our daily lives. Mobile computing is also on the rise, with 42 percent of customers in the United States owning smartphones at the end of 2011 (up 15 percent from 2010) (comScore 2012). Library users now expect libraries to have virtual library branches—avenues community members can use to access resources, services, and collections previously available only within the geo-library. The first step to developing a virtual library is creating a library website. Library websites and library mobile websites are building blocks of the virtual library. Each engages library patrons beyond the physical building and allows the library to travel with community members. By using free and low-cost platforms, website and mobile development can be done with a small investment of resources (time and money) by individuals with very few technical skills. So what are you waiting for? Get started building your virtual library!

REFERENCES

comScore, Inc. 2012. "U.S. Digital Future In Focus 2012: Key Insights from 2011 and What They Mean For the Coming Year." www.comscore.com/Press_Events/ Presentations_Whitepapers/2012/2012_US_Digital_Future_in_Focus.

Wolfram Research. 2011. WolframAlpha Computational Knowledge Engine. www.wolframalpha.com/input/?i=number+personal+computers+worldwide.

Social Media and Social Networking

Rene J. Erlandson

What is social media? What is social networking? Why should librarians care about either? Even if librarians and library users are not able to define the terms, when asked to give examples of social media or social networking venues, most quickly respond with sites like Facebook, Myspace, Twitter, Flickr, and You-Tube. The terms *social media* and *social networking* are often used interchangeably in conversation. However, for the purpose of this chapter, social media refers to channels of electronic communication used to create and distribute content that allows for interaction between content creator and end users—like blogs and wikis. Social networking refers to online sites where members exchange information, ideas, personal messages, and content—like Facebook and Twitter. Social media is content centered, while social networking focuses on connections people make online to form communities.

Now, why should librarians care about social media and social networking? At their core, libraries exist to facilitate information exchange within communities. Libraries connect community members with information. Just as librarians in the past used newsletters and e-mails to communicate with community members, blogs and new forms of social media can now be used to reach constituents. Librarians can also capitalize on the social networks of community members to transmit information and build new communities of support for libraries. In an era of shrinking library budgets and tough economic times, it is important to increase support for and awareness of libraries. Social media and social networking require a relatively small investment with the possibility of big rewards. However, as with any initiative, success is dependent on planning, commitment, and assessment.

SIX-STEP SOCIAL MEDIA AND SOCIAL NETWORKING INITIATIVE

This chapter is a step-by-step guide to successfully planning and developing a library presence on popular social networking platforms and creating and maintaining engaging library social media. By following the six steps outlined in this chapter, you will be able to create a manageable social media and social networking initiative for your library.

Define Project Goals and Objectives

The underlying motivation for creating social media or social networks often affects the success of the endeavor. If the goal of launching such an initiative is to keep up with peer institutions, the project is unlikely to succeed. The purpose of social networking is to make connections and create relationships that form a supportive community. Just as in real life, it takes time and energy to form relationships. Randomly calling and leaving messages on someone's voice mail periodically does not constitute a friendship; by the same token, creating a blog or Facebook page should not be the end goal of a social media and social network initiative.

Engagement is the key to success. For members of social networking platforms, their virtual communities are an extension of their physical communities. In order to establish and maintain social network connections, a presence must be interesting, supportive, or beneficial in some way. Library social media and social network presences that are not maintained do not benefit the community. A stagnant presence may be forgotten or, worse yet, dropped. Every broken connection is a missed opportunity to build support for the library. In extreme instances, unmaintained sites or pages within active online communities may damage the image of the library if community members feel the library does not care enough to engage with them. So it is important to carefully consider why you are launching a social networking initiative and how you will

> Begin to develop a social media and social network strategy by answering the following questions:
>
> Why are you are considering developing social media or a library presence on social networking platforms?
>
> What do you want to achieve with the initiative?

support and maintain the program over time before building a presence on any of the platforms.

Libraries also use social media and social networking platforms as tools to connect community members to general library information and services. Some social networking sites are useful in developing library-specific communities to support existing groups like readers' advisors, book clubs, and other programs. These sites also give the library a way to develop new programs for people who do not visit the library regularly, such as online only book clubs and reading programs. Other platforms allow developers to create platform-specific applications such as search widgets and library-related games that will further embed the library into the virtual lives of community members. Identifying the principal objectives of your library's social networking initiative will assist in determining which platform best suits your goals. Use the social networking strategy worksheet in figure 8.1 to create a list of specific objectives.

Allocate Project Resources

Once the principal objectives of the initiative are defined, allocate resources to support the initiative. Identify who will develop, implement, and maintain the initiative. Determine how much time will be committed to developing and maintaining the program. Specify the budget for the initiative, or lack thereof. Objectively considering resources to be allocated towards a social media and social networking initiative will assist in determining if you can sustain a long-term commitment to such a project.

It is possible to create Facebook and Twitter presences in under an hour by following the directions outlined later in this chapter. Once the accounts and pages are created, however, they must be maintained. While there are no rules to how much or how little time should be allocated to maintaining library social networking presences, consistency will provide the most success. Posting information regularly to Facebook, Twitter, blogs, etc., maintains an active library presence in the virtual lives of community members. However, there can be a fine line between being active and overdoing social networking activities at the risk of seeming intrusive or annoying to community members. So, begin with small steps; post once a day, two or three times a week, and build up to posting once a day five to seven times a week. Unless you are in a very active online community, like some college campuses or working with teenagers, limit posts to less than three a day. Also do not submit multiple posts in immediate succession. If posting more than once a day, break up

Why develop a library social media and social network presence?

What do you want to achieve by developing and implementing a library social media and social network initiative?

(promotion of_____; connect community members to_____;
support existing library related groups_____readers advisory, book clubs,
reading programs, library friends; . . .)

_____
Principle Objective 1:

_____
Principle Objective 2:

_____
Principle Objective 3:

_____
Principle Objective 4:

_____
What resources will be allocated towards the project?

Specific staff? _____

Development time? _____

Maintenance time?_____

Budget?_____

FIGURE 8.1
Social Media and Social Network Strategy Worksheet

the posts throughout the day. Utilizing these simple strategies will streamline the time needed to maintain library social media and network presences.

While all of the social networking presences outlined in this chapter are available for free by simply setting up an account, some platforms provide advertising possibilities and some have advanced features that may be subscribed to for a small fee. Please see specific platform sections of this chapter for details. Detailed information on developing social media presences can be found in the resources listed at the end of this chapter. In addition to direct costs like advertising and subscription fees, many libraries sponsor contests, drawings, and other competitions for community members where library promotional materials such as cups, earbuds, or flash drives are given away. So if you are planning to launch a promotion to give away library-related prizes, these indirect costs will need to be factored into the budget for the initiative.

Craft Social Media and Social Network Policy

Although social media and social networks are intended to facilitate communication between individuals, incorporation of both into the communication plans of organizations has created a blurring of lines between personal and professional employee interactions. Moreover, creating a virtual presence within communities many members consider personal may result in content being posted to library-sponsored sites that runs counter to acceptable conduct within the organization. In addition, because most social network sites do not regulate who creates sites within their platforms, it is possible for any library staff member to create a library presence without the knowledge of supervisors and administrators. If libraries want this process centralized to coordinate site aesthetics and make sure content reflects the library philosophy, this information needs to be communicated to staff as soon as possible. Therefore, as libraries develop social media and social networking initiatives, policies should be created to guide employee contacts and community member interactions within these platforms.

At the core, a social media and social networking policy is a basic rules-of-conduct statement for what is and is not acceptable behavior within a library-affiliated social platform. Most libraries have written conduct codes that govern behavior within the physical library building and statements for acceptable use of computers and electronic resources. A social media and social network policy often incorporates appropriate portions of the aforementioned documents. The length of policies may vary, but at the very least the document needs to clearly

_____ Library
Social Media and Social Network Policy

Social media and social networking platforms are powerful communication and community building tools. Social networking platforms are a viable means of developing a third place where community members may contribute to discussions and exchange information and ideas about aspects of education, the educational experience and institutions/organizations affiliated with higher education.

_____ Library recognizes the usefulness of developing social media content and participating in online social networking to fulfill the mission of the Library, connect community members to Library information, resources and services and to facilitate the sharing of ideas and opinions. Library-created social media content and participation within associated social networking platforms is guided by the same standards of civil discourse and behavioral standards, laws and professional expectations that govern interactions within the Library.

_____ Library reserves the right to modify or remove any messages, postings or comments to affiliated social-networking sites that include:

- all types of offensive language, including but not limited to obscene, racist, abusive, defamatory, and threatening
- pornographic or sexist references and images
- libelous and/or slanderous statements
- copyright and trademark violations
- personal information
- duplicate posts from the same individual
- images or other content that are off topic and/or do not relate to the library forum

Notwithstanding the foregoing, _____ Library is not obligated to take any such actions, and will not be responsible or liable for any interactions or content posted by any participant in any Library-affiliated social networking forum, event, or service. In addition, _____ Library does not endorse content outside that created by _____ Library staff. By using any _____ Library-related social networking services, participants agree to abide by the Social Media and Social Networking Policy and agree to indemnify the Library and its officers and employees, from and against all liabilities, judgments, damages, and costs (including attorney's fees) incurred which arise out of or are related to posted content.

FIGURE 8.2
Social Media and Social Network Policy Template

state what is considered unacceptable behavior and the possible ramifications of such behavior. A Google search of "library social media policy" provides links to many documents already in place for libraries across the country, where you can see common elements of such policies. In addition, the social media and social network policy template shown in figure 8.2 can be used to craft a policy in less than five minutes.

Select Social Media and Social Networking Platforms

Social media and social networking platforms facilitate communication, allowing people to share information and develop connections and relationships. With the number of social media and social networking options available, it can be difficult to decide where to invest time developing a library presence. However, simply stated, the library needs to be where community members are.

Facebook

With more than 500 million members who log in at least once a month, Facebook is by far the largest online social networking platform (Facebook 2011a, 2011b). Estimates are that 41 percent of people in the United States over the age of thirteen have a Facebook account. A quick way to find out a rough estimate of how many people in a given geographic area have Facebook accounts is to create a Facebook ad. Go to: www.facebook.com/advertising/ and click on the Create an Ad button. Accept all the defaults and type something into the body of the ad; then click the Continue button. The next screen allows you to target your ad based on country, state, city, age, etc. By targeting the ad to a specific geographic location you can discover how many members of Facebook live in your area. One caveat to this is Facebook does not verify account locations, so a member may list his or her home as San Diego but actually live in Peoria. However, the system-generated number gives a rough estimate of how many people in a specific geographic area can be reached with a Facebook Fan page (or ad).

Many libraries use Facebook to push information out to interested parties as well as to connect individuals with library collections, resources, and services. Through the Facebook application programming interface (API), libraries can develop library-specific Facebook applications that allow users to search the library catalog while in Facebook and connect to online library resources. Facebook pages can also target subsets of the larger library community—like a teen space, a readers' advisor page, or a book club page.

Blogs

While it is relatively easy to estimate potential connections within Facebook, that is not the case for other social media and social networking sites. However, it is useful to consider the format, features, membership, and appeal of other social media and social networking sites before beginning development. Weblogs, or blogs, date back to the 1990s. Most blogs today are hosted by free blogging platforms such as WordPress (http://wordpress.com) and Google's Blogger (www.blogger.com). Blogs are essentially websites where owners post information. There is no limit to the length of posts or to content. Blog posts can include images, video, audio, widgets, and games as well as text. RSS (Really Simple Syndication) feeds allow visitors to subscribe to an unlimited number of blogs with information of interest to an individual collated in one place via RSS readers like Google Reader and My Yahoo! Reader. Blogs allow library community members to access information produced by the library in a user-defined interface. WordPress claims that more than 357 million people throughout the world view 2.5 billion blog pages each month (wordPress.com 2012). Libraries often use blogs to push out information to community members about upcoming events and exhibits.

Twitter

Twitter is a real-time, microblogging platform that provides members with immediate access to short snippets of information called tweets. Twitter differs from regular blogs by limiting the length of a post to 140 characters. Members follow Twitter streams they find useful or interesting. Related information is linked through the use of hash tags (#), making it possible to see all the posts on a specific topic by searching for the topic hash tag. Twitter reports 145 million members worldwide (Shaer 2010). Due to the limited number of characters in a Tweet, Twitter is mainly useful for pushing out quick announcements about the library or news relevant to the community. Some libraries conduct contests via Twitter, like Tuesday Twitter Trivia, where the library posts a trivia question every Tuesday and the first person to answer correctly wins a prize that can be picked up at the library.

The three social media and social networking platforms described here represent a small percentage of all the platforms available. However, depending on desired objectives, each has the potential to reach a large number of community members with a small investment of resources.

Develop Presences

Once objectives are defined and media and platforms decided on, it is time to develop the library presence within the online community. Regardless of which platform you choose, initially you are creating a web page or pages within the platform. Features of the pages will vary depending on the development platform. So let's get started!

Facebook

While Facebook is the largest social network platform on the Web, it was created for individuals, not organizations. Therefore, before you can create a library fan page you must create a personal Facebook account to which the library page will be permanently linked. Facebook discourages alias accounts and will delete such an account if discovered, so an account must be associated with a real person. If you do not already have a Facebook account, go to www.facebook.com to create one. Think of developing a personal Facebook account as a dress rehearsal for creating the library site. You may add as much or as little information as you like to your personal profile. Don't forget to set your privacy settings and account settings under the Account link. The settings you establish for your personal profile are separate from the settings for the library page you will develop.

Once you have set up your Facebook account and profile, you will see a link to Create a Page at the bottom of your page, or go to www.facebook.com/pages/ and click on the Create Page button. Select Company, Organization, or Institution. Next you will need to choose a category for your organization. Unfortunately, Facebook does not have a separate category for libraries, so your best bet is to choose Government Organization, Nonprofit Organization, Education, University, or School, depending on the type of library you are creating a page for. Next, type in the name of your library in the Company Name box. Remember to check I Agree before clicking on the Get Started button.

Once you create the basic page, you may customize the page with images, links, and information. Whether developing a Facebook page for a small library or a large library, consider branding the page to complement the existing library web page or promotional materials. Create a face for the library by uploading a library logo or an image of the outside of the library building or some other recognizable library-associated image (a prominent work of art in the building, for example). An attractive, recognizable image quickly identifies the Facebook page with the library.

The Edit Page button links to a page from which a variety of settings can be updated. The Manage Permissions page allows one to define parameters for page

93

visibility, age restrictions, and a profanity block list. In addition, a page can be permanently deleted on the Manage Permissions page. By completing fields under Basic Information, general library information like address, phone number, main library website, and hours will be accessible via the new library Facebook page, Information link. As settings are edited, click on Save Changes to save settings and information. Click on View Page to see the updated Facebook page.

Many libraries use Facebook

Examples of successful library Facebook pages

Johnson County (KS) Library
www.facebook.com/jocolibrary

La Crosse Public Library
www.facebook.com/lacrosselibrary

New York Public Library
www.facebook.com/newyorkpublicli-brary

Skokie Public Library
www.facebook.com/skokielibrary

Topeka and Shawnee County Public Library
www.facebook.com/TopekaLibrary

to announce events happening at the library. Event pages are easily created by clicking on the Events link in the navigation bar and then clicking on the Create Event button. A template allows an event page to be created in a minute or two. Be sure to load a related image to the event page. It is also possible to send invitations to events via an events page, which hopefully supporters will repost to their friends.

Once the library page is set up, let community members know about it by importing e-mail addresses into Facebook and sending out a mass message to community members to let them know the library is now on Facebook. It is also possible to promote the new Facebook page from the main library website by adding a Like box. Go to the Like Button developer's page (http://developers.facebook.com/docs/reference/plugins/like). Fill in the information asked for in the developer widget and click on the Get Code button at the bottom of the widget to obtain the script for adding a Like box to the main library website.

Twitter

Unlike Facebook, Twitter allows businesses to establish accounts by simply going to http://twitter.com, entering a name, valid e-mail, and password. The system verifies the e-mail account and once the Create My Account button is clicked, an e-mail confirmation is sent to the e-mail account you supplied. Once again, it takes less than a minute to establish the account.

Once the library account is set up, go to the Settings pages to customize the look of the library Twitter site. The Settings pages use the Profile and Design tabs to customize the look of the library Twitter account. On the Design tab, Twitter supplies several background themes and color combi-

Examples of successful library Twitter pages:

Kansas City Public Library
http://twitter.com/#!/KCLibrary

McMaster University Libraries
http://twitter.com/#!/maclibraries

nations to choose from, or you can upload your own background image to create a totally customized look. Just as in Facebook, it is important to upload an image to the Profile page, so people can see the library. Use the library logo, or an image of the outside of the library for the profile picture that will display on the library Twitter page. Be consistent with the use of images and colors on all library sites to create a cohesive online environment for visitors. Also, be sure to include a link to the main library website and a description of the library in the biography (bio) field of the profile. Do not forget to click Save after editing the Profile page.

Blogs

Although there are many free platform options for developing a library blog, in this chapter we are going to walk through the process of developing a blog in Word-Press. To get started go to http://wordpress.com and click on the Get Started Here button. WordPress allows you to choose your blog address, so select an address easily associated with the library that visitors will remember. WordPress hosts addresses ending with wordpress.com for free (such as my-library.wordpress.com). If you prefer to have an address that is not associated with WordPress, there will be an annual charge for other .com, .org, and .net addresses (at time of publication $17 per year; check prices at https://en.wordpress.com/signup via the drop-down menu within the blog address field). Next select a username and password, associate the blog with an e-mail address, and select the blog posting language; then click on the Sign Up button. The system will send you a confirmation e-mail that you must respond to within forty-eight hours in order for the blog to be activated.

Once the blog is activated, it is time to customize the look of the blog. In the beginning, select one of the free two-column templates available within the platform. Go to the Blog Info tab and click on Theme. Browse through available templates and select one with a layout that appeals to you. Two-column layouts allow posted information to appear in the larger column, while the second smaller column is available to contain general library information, links to the library website, or widgets like the Facebook Like box. Template colors are easy to change by clicking on Appearance in the left navigation pane. From this page you may also upload a custom background image, select a specific background color, and upload a custom header. Creating a unique library blog is easy to do within WordPress.

The only thing left to do before the blog goes live is to consider the blog settings. Most default settings for a newly created blog within WordPress do not need to be altered; however, settings for fields that create metadata will need to be verified or edited. In addition, if you wish to moderate (approve) comments and discussion posts made to the blog, discussion settings will need to be altered. To edit fields used to create metadata, open the Dashboard via the My Blog tab to edit Settings. Complete, accurate metadata increases the chance people looking for information about the library will retrieve the blog when executing a Web search. Therefore it is important to verify the site title and enter a tagline that reflects the purpose of the blog—e.g., News and events for Prairieland College Library in Middletown, Illinois. After saving changes made to the information on this screen, upload an image to represent the blog. Next, edit discussion settings to reflect desired level of review. The Discussion Settings screen also provides a Comment Blacklist field that acts as a stop list for words entered into the field. Any posts/comments that contain blacklisted words will be marked as spam and held for review. Once all changes are saved, the blog is ready for the first post.

Maintain and Assess Success

Librarians who are considering implementing a social media or social networking initiative often want to know how much time they will need to devote to maintaining the site(s). This is a difficult question to answer because the amount of time needed to sustain an online social initiative depends on the goals and objectives identified for the project. If an objective is to provide reference assistance, readers' advisory assistance, or customer service through the initiative, then a significant amount of time every day may need to be

Maintenance Tips

- Be consistent.

- Post at least once a week.

- Post no more than three times a day.

- Spread posts throughout the day or week.

allocated to the initiative. However, if the goal is simply to engage with community members within a platform they already frequent, the sites can be successfully maintained in as little as an hour a week.

Approach maintenance of library social media and social networking sites systematically. Decide early on how many posts to make in a day or week. Be consistent. If posting every day is unrealistic, post every other day, or three times a week. If you decide to post three times a week, do not post three times within an hour and then not post anything else the rest of the week. Spread out posts over time so you do not flood fans and followers with library posts. If you are posting to Facebook, include images and videos that draw a viewer in. Upload pictures taken at library events or ask fans of the library to post pictures taken around the library.

Since developing social media and social networking sites in 2009 for the University of Nebraska Omaha Library, traffic, click-throughs, and comments have been tracked, indicating more people interact with the sites Tuesday through Thursday. Fall semester has the highest level of activity, and summer sessions have the lowest. Determining information that community members find interesting, and when they are most receptive to information from the library, can be used to target future communication. If possible, have more than one person post to the library sites. Distributing responsibility for maintaining sites disperses the work and can make the site more engaging by including differing perspectives and interests.

Regularly assess the impact of each platform presence over time. As new platforms emerge, community members migrate, so track the number of fans/followers and comments library sites receive over time. Five or six years ago many community members were on Myspace and few people had even heard of Facebook. So it is important to know where your community members are and to position the library accordingly.

CONCLUSION

Developing library social media and a library presence on social networking platforms engages community members in forms and venues they already frequent. By following the steps outlined in this chapter, you can easily create, maintain, and extend your virtual library presence. The keys to success are commitment, maintenance, assessment, and, above all, enjoyment. Have fun interacting with the people you connect with!

SOCIAL MEDIA AND SOCIAL NETWORKING RESOURCES

Handley, Ann and C.C. Chapman. 2011. *Content Rules: How to Create Killer Blogs, Podcasts, Videos, EBooks, Webinars (and More) that Engage Customers and Ignite Your Business.* Hoboken, NJ: John Wiley and Sons.

Landis, Cliff. 2010. *A Social Networking Primer for Librarians.* New York: Neal-Schuman.

Libert, Barry. 2010. *Social Nation.* Hoboken, NJ: John Wiley & Sons.

Safko, Lon. 2010. *The Social Media Bible: Tactics, Tools & Strategies for Business Success.* Hoboken, NJ: John Wiley & Sons.

Solomon, Laura. 2010. *Doing Social Media So It Matters: A Librarian's Guide.* Chicago: American Library Association.

REFERENCES

Facebook. 2011a. "Statistics." http://newsroom.fb.com/Key-Facts.

Facebook. 2011b. "Factsheet." http://newsroom.fb.com/Key-Facts.

Shaer, Matthew. 2010. "Twitter Founder: Twitter Will Hit One Billion Member Mark." *The Christian Science Monitor.* October 12. www.csmonitor.com/Innovation/Horizons/2010/1012/Twitter-founder-Twitter-will-hit-one-billion-member-mark.

WordPress.com. 2012. "Stats." http://en.wordpress.com/stats.

Open-Source Applications

Rachel A. Erb

There are many ways in which librarians can capitalize on the benefits of open-source software (OSS), but a working definition of the open-source (OS) concept is essential before we proceed. Technically speaking, open source refers to an application in which the source code is available for the general public to use and modify without any cost to the user. In most instances, open source is a collaborative effort among programmers to improve the code and share their efforts for the benefit of others in the open-source community.

Open source had its origins in the technological community in response to the restrictions and limitations of customizing commercial proprietary software. Developers began creating free and customizable products for the benefit of the user community. As a result, many OS analogs are commonly used commercial software products. For example, the Open Office suite of software products is an OS analog for the popularly used Microsoft Office suite, including analogs for Word, Excel, etc. Although the user with a programming background can modify many OS programs, it is not necessary to be a programmer in order to use and benefit from these applications in their native form. In fact, you probably use many OS applications without realizing that they are open source. For instance, Google's e-mail application, Gmail, is considered to be open-source software.

Many librarians in small and solo operations may be unsure if there is any potential utility for OS in their work environments. We will demonstrate that there are many OS applications that are quite useful for library services and that can assist with daily operations. Perceived lack of technical acumen or support should not be a deterrent to implementing open-source software. The criteria for an open-source software product's inclusion within this chapter are potential utility to a library's operations and ease of installation. Although there are many other excellent open-source applications, they were excluded from this examination because they require either programming skills to implement, access to a server, or have complicated installation requirements. Furthermore, there is a steady stream of new OS applications offered to the public. It would be nearly impossible to include all of them for your consideration, but a basic overview of some of the OS applications that are currently available will help you become familiar with their utility and potential.

PROJECT MANAGEMENT

In smaller and solo operations librarians generally assume multiple roles and are juggling several projects at any given time. Fortunately, there are OSS applications that will assist librarians with managing numerous projects with differing levels of complexity and deadlines.

OpenProj

OpenProj (http://openproj.org) was developed as a free alternative to Microsoft Project. It is fairly intuitive, requiring little time from downloading the product to quickly creating a project. As with Microsoft Project, the user can add tasks, set the duration for a project with a start and completion date, define predecessors, and assign resources. OpenProj offers numerous modes for viewing a project:

- Gantt chart
- Network diagram
- Resource view
- Projects view
- Work breakdown structure chart
- Resource breakdown structure chart
- Report view (generates printable reports)
- Task usage detail
- Resource usage detail
- Histogram (provides detailed, graphical view of resource assignments; this is useful for monitoring resource allocation)

This product requires desktop installation. It is compatible with most operating environments such as Windows, Mac OS, and Linux. Before installation make sure that Sun Java Runtime Environment version 1.5 or later is running on your desktop. Once the installation of Sun Java Runtime is either confirmed or completed, you can install OpenProj by clicking on Download Now. Then, there will be a prompt to download the msi file to a directory of your choice.

Documentation is provided via wiki. The wiki is frequently updated to reflect each version's subsequent modifications. While not currently complete, the documentation is substantial enough for the user to begin creating projects with the application.

OpenProj is ideal for both novice users and experienced project managers alike. As a desktop application, it is currently the closest analog to Microsoft Project. While it does lack some of the more advanced features of Microsoft Project, it is surprisingly robust and flexible.

iTeamwork

Open-source software applications hosted in the cloud are a burgeoning trend. One of the more popular choices is long-standing iTeamwork (www.iteamwork.com). iTeamwork is a web-based team product management system. It allows project managers to break down complex projects into tasks that can be assigned to other participants. Collaboration with colleagues in other locations is very simple because iTeamwork employs e-mail as its notification system. Likewise, the project manager can also use e-mail in order to receive an outline of all incomplete tasks and tasks that were not completed by the deadline.

Creating a project requires a project name and a target completion date. Once the project is created, the project manager or team members can add tasks, which can include detailed annotations. As tasks are in progress, the project manager can view the percentage completed and modify or delete them.

As software-as-a-service (SaaS), the software does not require installation. Registration is a simple process, requiring minimal personal information such as a username and password. There is also a link to a user guide which is detailed enough to get started using this product rather quickly.

In summary, iTeamwork has an extremely short learning curve and is very intuitive. This makes it a suitable application for those who cannot devote time to learning OpenProj. As a basic product, it is ideal for the project manager who does not need project management software with extensive and complex features.

LessProjects, Dooster, and Manymoon

There are a few other project management software products that are more sophisticated than iTeamwork and do not require downloading. Two notable examples are LessProjects (http://lessprojects.com) and Dooster (http://dooster.net). LessProjects is excellent for managing individual tasks. You can prioritize, assign tasks to users, and manage multiple projects. Dooster is another basic online project management software product that is easy to use. It lacks some of the advanced features of LessProjects, but it is suitable for team collaboration and task creation and assignation. What is noteworthy about Dooster is its compatibility with mobile technology devices.

Google aficionados will appreciate Manymoon (http://manymoon.com), which fully integrates with Google applications such as Google Docs and Google Calendar. At publication time, Google does not offer a project management web application. While Manymoon does not offer advanced features such as Gantt charts, it provides a solution for those using Google's applications.

Project management does not have to be an arduous feat with so many free software options. There are many choices, which can make it difficult to select a product. If it is not possible to download OpenProj, then try some of the aforementioned options in the cloud. Keep in mind, the development of project management OSS will continue to increase and there will be even more products available over time.

SCREENCASTING

Many OSS applications create screencasts that can be used for demonstrations and tutorials. Most of these products require minimal to no video production skills. Also, it is possible to create your first screencast within a matter of minutes.

Screencasting: Planning

StoryBoard Pro

StoryBoard Pro (www.atomiclearning.com/storyboardpro) is a preproduction tool for video and screencast projects. This software was designed for educators and uses the FileMaker Pro runtime engine. This desktop application is compatible with both Windows and Macintosh operating systems.

StoryBoard Pro is simple to use. Its key features allow the user to create a comprehensive storyboard. The user can perform any of the following tasks:

- Enter titles and descriptions of sections, including planned length.
- Indicate shot types such as video, still and audio.
- Enter screencasting tips such as panning.
- Import existing video clips.
- Create templates for video projects.
- Print copies of the storyboard to use while filming and editing.

StoryBoard Pro is ideal to use for screencasts that introduce several concepts or procedural steps within a tutorial. It does lack illustration features that are available in commercial products, but this is not necessary for those who simply need a basic planning utility. The novice will be able to create a storyboard resulting in a successful screencast or video production.

Screencasting: Software

Webinaria

Webinaria (www.webinaria.com) is basic screen capturing software for the Microsoft Windows operating system. This software works well for creating three to five minute tutorials that illustrate one concept. You can capture either the entire screen or just a portion of the screen. The video can be saved as either avi or flv file formats. The most current version, Webinaria 2.1, includes a video editor that allows users to edit screencasts by selecting frames on a timeline. After the screencast is completed, files are hosted and stored on webinaria.com. The screencasts can be shared via e-mail links from the site and can also be embedded in other websites. Webinaria is ideal for quick, focused tutorials that require little editing.

CamStudio

CamStudio (http://camstudio.org) is another free screen capturing software application that is only compatible with the Windows operating system. This software records screencasts from your desktop in avi and swf file formats. The program has some audio and video options, such as recording with accompanying sound and automatically panning. It is also possible to include annotated comments within the frames. Despite these features, the program lacks a basic editing component.

CamStudio does not offer screencast hosting, so the screencasts must be stored locally and embedded in a website. Like Webinaria, CamStudio is another software product that is suitable for quick tutorials. The creator is limited to avi and swf files because other types of files are not supported.

Jing

Jing (www.techsmith.com/jing), on the other hand, is screen-casting software that is compatible with both Windows and Mac operating systems. Screen recordings are made in swf file format and can be saved to a desktop, an FTP server, or on screencast.com (2 GB free storage). It is also possible to include an audio voiceover while recording. Jing's screen captures are customizable according to common screen measurements, but that is the extent of its dynamic features. Also, Jing has no editing features. Despite its limited flexibility, Jing is very effective for simple screencasts that are no longer than five minutes. The capability of hosting screencasts on screencast.com for free allows for quick and simple sharing with others.

Screencasting: Video Editing

Many of the previously reviewed open-source screencast software products lack editing capabilities. There are, however, a few freeware video editing applications that are available and compatible with many of the common screencast file formats previously cited in this chapter. Paired with video production software, these applications are very effective in generating quality screencasts.

Avidemux

Avidemux (http://fixounet.free.fr/avidemux) is powerful video editing software that is compatible with most operating systems. Avidemux is intuitive to use, yet very effective for quickly editing videocasts. Avidemux facilitates cropping, re-encoding, and user-defined filtering. This program is suitable for many video formats including flv, mpeg, avi, vcd, h.263/4, as well as audio formats such as mp3, acc, ogg, vorbis, and wav. Avidemux is one of the more sophisticated open-source video editing software programs to date.

SolveigMM AVI Trimmer

Another editing program that is more basic is SolveigMM AVI Trimmer (www .solveigmm.com/?Products&id=AVITrimmer). Primarily employed for avi editing, it is unencumbered by encoding/decoding processes. All file sizes are supported. SolveigMM AVI Trimmer can be fully integrated with Windows Media Player as a plug-in.

SolveigMM AVI Trimmer is simple to use and recommended if the more comprehensive features of Avidemux are not necessary for the project at hand. One potential challenge is this program is not consistently effective in truncating the initial several seconds of an avi file. This is not a problem, however, for cropping anywhere in the middle or end of the file.

CONTENT MANAGEMENT SYSTEMS (CMS)

Vosao

Vosao (www.vosao.org) is the first free content management system that is hosted in the cloud. The project began in 2009 in order to create an open-source CMS for free site hosting on the Google App Engine. The installation process is refreshingly straightforward: from Vosao's site, prospective users must request installation, which will result in the latest stable version being installed to a new Google App site. Upon notification of installation, users can begin to create and manage a site with a web browser.

Beginning to build a site is quite simple. Web authorizing skills are not required to create websites with Vosao because it features a visual (WYSIWYG) editor. Other features that point to Vosao's ease of use are: the parent-child page system, prenested and configurable templates, site import and export, security and group management, several plug-ins, and free hosting in the Google cloud. Therefore, Vosao CMS is highly recommended for those who need to create and manage a basic website but do not have server access. This CMS is far less intimidating than, and as effective as, many systems that require a server and requisite programming skills.

105

CMS Made Simple

CMS Made Simple (www.cmsmadesimple.org) is an open-source content management system built using PHP and designed for those who wish to build small semi-static websites. The CMS Made Simple website offers hundreds of free templates and many of them are designed for the corporate and organization environment. This software includes a few core modules that are part of the installation package such as a search function, WYSIWIG editor, form builder, newsletter, and Google site map. There are also hundreds of add-on modules available for downloading and installation directly from the CMS Made Simple website.

Even though it is not essential to have any knowledge of PHP prior to installation, there is a bit of a learning curve for successful use of this software. One must understand certain basic principles before working with CMS Made Simple, including basic concepts of database creation and maintenance, FTP to a remote host, HTML, and CSS.

For desktop hosting, CMS Made Simple also requires WAMP and Apache, MySQL, and PHP or the Windows environment. The most stable installation site is WAMP Server (www.wampserver.com/en).

There is also community technical support for this software. The CMS Made Simple forum boasts a very active group of users willing to provide assistance. In addition, members of the development team participate in the forum. Most problems can be solved by seeking assistance via the CMS Made Simple forum. If you find it necessary to have ongoing support, CMS Made Simple offers commercial support for a fee.

CushyCMS and PageLime

CushyCMS (www.cushycms.com/en) is another CSM hosted in the cloud. Basic accounts are free and pro-accounts are approximately $30 per month. Pro-accounts allow extensive customization and branding. Similar to CushCMS, PageLime (www.pagelime.com) is hosted in the cloud and is very easy to use. PageLime offers three free sites and has a pricing scale based on the number of sites a user maintains.

There are plenty of free CMSs available for those without server access. The widespread availability of CMSs hosted in the cloud make it possible for quick and easy website development.

SUBJECT GUIDES

There are many open-source software applications that can perform double duty as library subject guides including CMSs, wikis, blogs, and course management software. For many smaller libraries any of these applications will be sufficient for creating subject guides. There are some excellent open-source library subject guides, but many of them require substantial technical support as well as some programming knowledge in order to effectively implement and support. There is one, however, that was designed with the ease of installation in mind—SubjectsPlus can be installed from a desktop with a few preliminary desktop installations.

Developed at Ithaca College, SubjectsPlus (www.subjectsplus.com) is an open-source application that offers several modules, which are useful for library services. The subject guide layout includes the ability to link to relevant electronic resources, offer second or third party RSS feeds, and embedded screencasts, among other features. SubjectPlus is ideal for creating subject or course guides, but its other modules are briefly noted:

- A–Z list of databases
- FAQs
- Suggestion box (aka TalkBack)
- Staff list

The system requirements for SubjectsPlus may seem daunting; you will need a web server with MySQL (greater than 4.1) and PHP (greater than 4, preferably greater than 5). Do not let this dissuade you from considering this application. The SubjectsPlus download site has several detailed tutorials regarding all system requirements, but what follows is a quick overview of what this will entail in order to satisfy these requirements.

MySQL and PHP can be installed on one's desktop (www.wampserver.com/en). First install WAMP (Apache, MySQL, and PHP for the Windows environment). Then install phpMyAdmin on your desktop. This solution works only if you have administrative rights for installing software on your PC. If you lack these rights, create a web server on a stick! This involves downloading the software to and running applications from a USB drive. MoWeS Portable (www.chsoftware .net/en/mowes/mowesportable/mowes.htm) works with most Windows computers and you do not have to install anything on your PC or modify its registry. If installation is still problematic, there is a very active support group that can assist with troubleshooting.

SubjectsPlus is comparable to other commercial and more complex library subject guides. It is even flexible enough to serve as a small library's content management system. For those reasons, it is highly recommended.

WIKIS

There are so many hosted wiki platforms to choose from it is nearly impossible to select a few that are optimal for the small library environment. Whichever wiki platform is selected for your library's needs, it should be simple to implement. Unlike MediaWiki, which requires installation, your hosted wiki can be up and running within a matter of minutes.

Wikimatrix

Narrowing wiki options to only software-as-a-service packages still leaves prospective users with a formidable list for selection. There is, however, a wiki selection tool, Wikimatrix (www.wikimatrix.org), which generates user-initiated comparison charts from the menu. By selecting the Wiki Choice Wizard, it is possible to limit your selection to only hosted options. Intended for those with scant to no wiki experience, all of the limiting options are presented with as little technical language as possible. Another way to use Wikimatrix is to select from the list of wikis and generate a custom comparison chart. The charts disclose many features of the wikis including system requirements, hosting features (specifically, bandwidth quota), security, development and support, output (HTML, CSS, mobile friendly, etc.), media file integration, and syntax examples.

LEARNING MANAGEMENT SYSTEMS (LMS)

As with wikis and content management systems, there are many choices for open-source course management systems. LMSs lend themselves to being effective library subject guides and have been employed for that purpose. Most of them, including the ones listed here, are excellent options for creating course and library subject guides. Many of them require WAMP installation. Despite this, they are worth briefly noting here:

- Moodle (http://moodle.org)
- ATutor (http://atutor.ca)
- Dokeos (www.dokeos.com)
- Claroline (www.claroline.net)

At publication time, there are two known services that offer free Moodle hosting:

- NineHub (http://ninehub.com)
- e-Socrates (www.e-socrates.org)

These hosted applications only require registration for course creation. They are highly recommended if WAMP installation remains an obstacle.

SURVEYS

The choices of open-source survey products can be overwhelming. Because many of them differ in offered features, it is essential to examine each product carefully before selecting one. In some cases, developers offer an additional subscription-based product that has more comprehensive features than the free version. What follows is a list of some free survey tools that permit more than ten questions per survey but may have other restrictions.

LimeSurvey

LimeSurvey (www.limesurvey.org) is not a desktop application, but one that has several server requirements that would be very difficult for the novice to implement. Some users successfully installed LimeSurvey on a PC, but documentation is currently lacking. LimeService (www.limeservice.com), however, is a free-hosted version of LimeSurvey. While LimeService has the same features as LimeSurvey, twenty-five responses from survey participants per month are free. The costs per each additional response are currently not disclosed on this website, but one hundred responses purchased in advance is $10. The cost per response declines as the number of responses purchased in advance increases (the limit is 5,000).

It would be impossible to enumerate all of LimeService's features, but here is a truncated list of some important things it can create.

- Unlimited number of surveys at the same time
- Unlimited number of questions in a survey (only limited by your database)
- Unlimited number of participants in a survey
- Twenty different question types
- Conditions for questions depending on earlier answers
- Reusable editable answer sets
- Assessment surveys
- Anonymous and non-anonymous surveys
- Enhanced import and export functions to text, CSV, PDF, SPSS, queXML (open-source XML schema for designing questionnaires), and MS Excel format

If cost is an issue and the survey population is less than twenty-five, then LimeService is a fine option.

KwikSurveys

KwikSurveys (www.kwiksurveys.com) is another free web-based survey tool. KwikSurveys is one of the most robust, free survey tools currently available. One of the main differences between KwikSurveys and LimeService is that KwikSurveys offers an unlimited number of respondents free of charge. Following are some of its other features:

- Unlimited number of questions and surveys
- Question builder
- Skip logic
- Ability to download to MS Word or Open Office
- Ability to export results to any spreadsheet program
- Filter responses

A WORD ABOUT GOOGLE

Google offers many free applications that address the technological needs of the library environment—all it requires is a few minutes to create a free account. There are several popular and highly regarded Google applications such as Gmail, Google's e-mail application that has similar functionality to Microsoft Exchange or Lotus Notes; Google Calendar, which allows the user to create calendars and share them with others; Google Docs, which enables the creation of word documents, spreadsheets, and presentations in collaboration with other users; and Google Reader, an RSS feed reader that also allows sharing of feeds with users.

The ever-expanding Google suite of applications is worth monitoring. This is underscored by the fact that Google is committed to ensuring most applications used in educational environments are free. A good place to begin would be Google's website, Google Apps for Education (www.google.com/apps/intl/en/edu) because it offers an overview of these applications as well as ideas on how they might be employed in an educational setting.

CONCLUSION

As illustrated, there are many open-source applications that are not only useful for smaller library operations, but are also relatively simple to implement. Fortunately, the number of OS software programs continues to grow and there are many more that lend themselves to exploration. Be confident that you can take advantage of the technology options that open-source software can provide to improve and simplify library operations.

Further OSS Exploration

Keeping up with developments in the OSS arena can be overwhelming, but there are some outstanding resources that can assist with discovering current information:

Open Source as Alternative
www.osalt.com

OSDir.com
http://osdir.com

OSS Watch
www.oss-watch.ac.uk

The Open Road
http://news.cnet.com/openroad

ZDNet Open Source
www.zdnet.com/blog/open-source

Digital Collections

Nicci Westbrook

With the rapidly changing technology in the field of digital collections, it may seem impractical to create unique digital collections at small and one-person libraries. However, with careful project planning and critical examination of current practices it is possible to organize successful small scale digitization initiatives. Such digitization projects make it possible to share hidden gems of unique local or niche collections that are valuable to the immediate library community and the world. This chapter pinpoints critical aspects of digital collection creation, publication, preservation, marketing, and assessment. Robust standards and practices for each stage in the digital collection life cycle are outlined as well as ways to practically scale industry standards to allow for limited staff and budgets.

THINKING GLOBALLY ABOUT DIGITAL COLLECTIONS

When considering a digital project, it is important to envision the entire digital collection life cycle from selection, digitization, and publication to preservation, marketing, and assessment before beginning work. Prior to launching a digitization initiative, consider resources that will be needed to successfully complete the project. Will equipment need to be purchased? Will staff need training? How much time will be allocated toward completing the initiative? How will digitized materials be delivered to patrons? Who will create metadata and what standards will they use? Will collection owners wish to review metadata before publication? These questions will shape a detailed project plan which will help library staff overcome potential roadblocks and successfully complete the project.

Once a project plan is formed, it is important to share this plan with potential stakeholders. Regardless of library size, digital collection initiatives need initial and continued support from stakeholders to succeed. Be sure to solicit buy in from the library director or governing board early in the process. If supervisors or peers are not convinced of the value of digital collections, projects can stall before they even begin. Is there a friends group who might be willing to support the project financially? Digitization projects entail both up front and ongoing costs. Finally, building general excitement around potential digitization projects among internal stakeholders and patrons can provide the necessary momentum to establish ongoing digitization efforts and ensure that the projects produced are well used.

SELECTING MATERIALS TO DIGITIZE

Most digital projects stem from a desire to provide online access to analog materials. Identifying materials for digitization can be one of the most exciting and challenging tasks associated with creating digital collections. While at first glance, partnering with collection owners might not seem to be an issue for small or one-person libraries wishing only to digitize a selection of their own materials, most digitization projects are collaborative to some degree. Depending on library size, the person responsible for digitization might not be the administrator of the analog materials identified for inclusion in the project. Additionally, external partnerships with local cultural heritage institutions can be an opportunity to share valuable historical materials beyond the library collection with patrons and build collaborative relationships with other community organizations.

Whether a library is partnering with internal or external collection owners, written documentation of collection development policies, including detailed explanation of selection criteria, can help staff make decisions about what materials should be digitized and how to prioritize backlogs.

Selection Criteria for Materials to Digitize

- rareness
- condition
- use
- equipment capabilities
- budget limitations
- copyright

Rareness, condition, use, equipment capabilities, budget limitations, and copyright are common digitization selection criteria.

First, the rareness of the material itself—is the item one of only a handful of surviving copies of a book or pamphlet? Is the item unique? The second aspect of rareness that plays a role in selection criteria is whether the item is rare among digital collections. If only two copies of a rare book are cataloged in WorldCat, the item itself might be considered rare. However, if one of the copies has already been competently digitized and is freely available, the value of duplicating that work would be questionable. The condition of the material might also drive prioritization for digitization. If the item is deteriorating rapidly, such that the content might not be available in the near future, it might rise to the top of the priority list. However, if the condition of the item is so poor that expensive preservation work would be required before digitization could safely occur, digitization plans for that item might have to be placed on hold. If available, usage statistics or anecdotal information from collection owners can inform which items should be digitized based on use. There will also be materials that simply cannot easily be digitized using the equipment available. Many rare books, for instance cannot be digitized facedown on flatbed scanners without damage to their spines. Finally, general budget constraints might inform which materials can be digitized and in what order. Although a collection might contain 3,000 historic photographs, the budget may allow for digitization of only 1,000 images. Conversely, if a friends group or donor gives money in support of one set of items over another, that collection might trump other materials slated for digitization. The above criteria are only a few of many factors that influence whether items will be digitized and if so in what order. Regardless of the specifics of selection criteria, the important thing is to create a decision matrix to guide objective discussion of project or item prioritization.

Few library staff consider themselves experts on copyright law. However, it is prudent to consider copyright when selecting materials for digitization, creating born-digital collections, and accepting donations from members of the community. While the legalities of copyright for digital library materials are complex, there are basic guidelines library staff can use to make informed decisions about copyright in regards to digitization projects. Foremost, if your institution has access to legal counsel either through your library or a larger state or private entity, consult with these individuals first. In the absence of professional legal counsel, research current copyright rules as they pertain to publication of digital library items, use conservative judgment, and publish items in good faith. When accepting born-digital

Copyright Resources

Copyright Navigator (http://navigator.carolon.net)—This visual, interactive resource illustrates the fundamentals of copyright law as they pertain to different types of materials.

Copyright Slider (http://librarycopyright.net/resources/digitalslider)—This slider allows the user to select the type of material at hand and returns an easy-to-understand explanation of the copyright status of that item for works published in the United States.

Cornell Copyright Information Center (http://copyright.cornell.edu)—This resource offers the same information as the Copyright Slider but is formatted differently and contains useful bibliographic material at the bottom.

Stanford Copyright Renewal Database (http://collections.stanford.edu/copyrightrenewals/bin/page?forward=home)—This database makes searchable the copyright renewal records received by the US Copyright Office between 1950 and 1992 for books published in the U.S. between 1923 and 1963. The database includes only U.S. Class A (book) renewals.

materials or analog donations from members of the community, consider adding a section to your donor agreement form that stipulates permission to publish the materials online.

SELECTING A FREE OR LOW-COST PLATFORM FOR CONTENT DELIVERY

Once materials to be digitized are identified, it is prudent to begin selecting a content delivery system. If possible, a content delivery platform should be selected before other equipment and workflow decisions are in place because much of the work of digital collection creation will flow naturally from the functionality of the platform chosen. There are many factors to consider when selecting a content delivery system, including patron interface, back-end interface, digital object display capabilities, metadata capabilities, support (from a company or a community of users), and long-term stability.

Patron interface may very well be the most important factor to evaluate when selecting a content delivery system. Ease of use and attractiveness of the front-end interface can directly impact traffic to digital collections and overall user satisfaction. In addition to appraising whether the patron interface is intuitive and appealing, consider whether it is easy to customize. With this and other facets of the content delivery system, it is important to determine the degree of staff expertise needed to achieve the desired outcome. The quality of the back-end interface also relates to staff expertise. If staff are not technology experts, selecting a system with a simple, straightforward upload, metadata, and publishing interface might be a priority.

Digital object display capability is related to two other factors: selection of materials and selection of equipment. For this reason, it sometimes helps to have a general idea of what materials will be digitized before considering content delivery systems. For instance, if audiovisual content is slated for digitization, it is important to select a content delivery system that can capably handle common audiovisual file formats.

As the field of digital libraries has grown, the number of metadata schemas commonly attached to digital items has diversified rather than streamlined. As such, if metadata staff at your institution prefer one schema over another, ensure that the content delivery system selected accommodates this schema. Likewise, certain metadata schemas are appropriate for certain media, so consider whether the content delivery system can support the metadata schemas that are most commonly used for the types of items selected for digitization. It is also important to consider how much control library staff will have over the functionality of metadata fields. Can staff control which fields are visible to users? Can staff create and format local fields if needed?

Finally, make sure to evaluate support and long-term stability of the content delivery system. Some products offer professional support that is included in the purchase price, while others offer support in the form of community forums only. It is also wise to select a content delivery system that is likely to be available for the foreseeable future. If many large institutions use the same system, it is unlikely that the system will disappear overnight. Selecting a stable system can prevent the need to migrate digital files and metadata content in the event of content delivery system obsolescence. Once again, staff expertise in system support will determine the threshold levels to expect from a viable content delivery system.

While the number of content delivery systems suited to small or one-person libraries is growing, at the time of writing there are three free or low-cost options that are commonly used: Omeka, CONTENTdm Quick Start, and Flickr. Omeka is a free, open-source content delivery system commonly used by museums, libraries,

Things to Consider When Selecting a Content Delivery System

- patron interface
- back-end interface
- digital object display capabilities
- metadata capabilities
- support
- long-term stability

and other cultural heritage institutions. It has a free sandbox feature that allows potential users to try out the back-end and front-end interfaces before installation so library staff can evaluate whether they meet identified criteria. Where content delivery systems are concerned, Omeka has fairly standard patron interface, back-end interface, and metadata capabilities—including many of the most commonly used schemas. Because Omeka is open source, questions of support and longevity of the product remain a concern, but concerns are mitigated by the presence of a strong user community. This is also reflected in the fact that Omeka offers several hosted options at subscription rates ranging from $49-$1,000 per year.

CONTENTdm is an OCLC product that works much like Omeka. Full instances of CONTENTdm can be expensive, but there is a Quick Start option for OCLC FirstSearch subscribers that allows institutions to publish up to three collections totaling 3,000 items. On one hand, user support and longevity are less of a concern than with Omeka as OCLC is a longstanding institution. However, if budget constraints dictate use of a free content delivery system that will support more than 3,000 items, Omeka or Flickr might be appropriate choices.

Flickr is by far the least expensive and easiest to use of the three systems. Furthermore, if your institution is able to gain entry into the Flickr Commons group, exposure of your images to a large audience is likely. The major downside of Flickr as a content delivery system is the lack of customization options with the patron interface and the informality of metadata within the system. However, many larger institutions have designed creative metadata solutions for digital objects in Flickr and are often willing to share code. Another drawback to Flickr is that it is intended for use as an image archive and is not as well suited for display of text documents.

EQUIPMENT AND SOFTWARE

Once a content delivery system is chosen, digitization equipment and software can be selected. Digitization is one of the most important—and often the most costly—aspects of digital collection projects. Whenever possible, purchased digitization equipment should have the capacity to handle materials currently selected for digitization as well as projected future projects. This section highlights equipment and software options for digitization of images, audio, and multimedia materials.

The two most common options for creating digital images of photographs, documents, or books are cameras and scanners. Both come in a wide variety of sizes, costs, and capabilities. While fully stocked digital labs might boast an assortment of each, a small or one-person library could digitize most materials with clever use of either a camera or a scanner. A high-quality digital SLR mounted on a simple camera stand can be used to create access and preservation images of photographs, books, and three-dimensional objects. Some also have video capabilities that might be useful for creating content or promotional videos for digital collections.

When selecting digital cameras, there are several things to consider. Perhaps the most important criterion is a low signal-to-noise ratio. If you are able to control the lighting conditions in your digitization space, a low signal-to-noise ratio will ensure that the resulting images will be clearer. Second, consider image sensor size. Look for a digital camera with an image sensor that is at least sixteen megapixels, especially if library staff or patrons might like to enlarge images to poster size for promotion or display. Finally, if your institution has already purchased a camera with lenses, consider sticking with the same brand. Lenses constitute a significant portion of the cost of high-quality cameras. Therefore, as the camera body becomes obsolete or as more cameras are added to a library's arsenal, lenses can be shared and reused for a considerable cost saving.

A camera purchase is fairly straightforward, but the diversity of scanners can be overwhelming. If your budget allows for purchase of only one scanner, consider an orbital scanner that can capture flat objects, books, and some three-dimensional materials. Orbital scanners capture an image from above, which ensures that the face of the image need not be flattened against a scanning surface. They also capture slight dimensionality. Low-relief, three-dimensional objects can be captured—scrapbooks, costumes, etc.—though imaging in the round is best left to cameras. If your budget allows for purchase of a second scanner, consider purchasing either a flatbed scanner with transparency capabilities—for capture of slides, photonegatives, etc.—or a scanner with document feed technology if the materials you intend to digitize are not fragile.

Once you have captured digital images, at least minor processing will be needed. Industry standard is Adobe Photoshop, which is a powerful though costly option. Increasingly, there are low-cost alternatives that can accommodate basic editing

119

needs of digital library workflows. Photoshop Elements is a low-cost light version of Adobe Photoshop. There are also two free programs that are quite good—GIMP and Aviary.

Audio and multimedia capture and editing is an emerging area of digital collections,-which makes it difficult to identify the exact tools an average lab might contain. However, it is important to carefully consider the type of audio, video, or other materials to be digitized and then thoroughly research equipment alternatives. Depending on your project, the cost might be less if audio or multimedia digitization is outsourced. If you outsource materials, be certain to establish a quality control workflow for accepting the digitized materials to ensure that all digitized content received is playable and of the expected quality.

The equipment and software described here require a high level of technical competency to operate effectively. However, allowing staff time to become familiar with new equipment and using the robust documentation materials available for products outlined here may be all that is needed to establish workflows. If more advanced training is needed, look for online forums associated with selected equipment and software. Reaching out to neighboring institutions using the same equipment and software can also yield unexpected advanced training opportunities at little or no cost.

STANDARDS

Purchasing equipment and using it competently is not enough to ensure the digitized items created will be appropriate for long-term access and preservation. Digitization standards for images, audio, and multimedia are still evolving, but industry practice is described here. Most digital libraries tend to operate in terms of preservation files and access files. Preservation files should be captured in a way that entails the least amount of processing your devices and software allow. When working with images, preservation files often extend slightly beyond the item itself—to capture borders—and may contain targets such as a WhiBal card or Gretag Macbeth ColorChecker that can be used for color matching for print if necessary. Most libraries capture 600 DPI uncompressed TIFF files for preservation. Consider the ongoing budget of your digitization plan and the price of storage when deciding whether to capture lower resolution files or use compressed files for preservation.

From the preservation file, one derivative file is usually created for access—this is the version that will be published on the Web for patrons to view. In this version, all of the borders can be cropped and minor editing can be performed—though most institutions subscribe to the notion that the digitized file should represent the original as accurately as possible and imperfections in the original should be left as is. Most libraries use 300 DPI JPEG files for access, though if storage is an issue, you might consider going as low as 72 DPI—fine quality resolution for the Web—provided you are keeping high-quality preservation files. If library staff or patrons are likely to use your images for publication in their research or for print projects such as posters or flyers, consider keeping at least 240 DPI files, which is the minimum acceptable size for print quality. While JPEG files remain the most commonly used access file type, some institutions are beginning to experiment with JPEG 2000 files for access. Whatever resolutions and file types you choose, it is essential to establish workflow that includes standards that are as robust as possible while fitting within budget and digitization capabilities.

In addition to digitization standards, the metadata created to describe digitized items should also adhere to set standards. The most common metadata schemas used for digital items are VRA Core, Dublin Core, and MODS. VRA Core is designed specifically for visual collections, while Dublin Core can be thought of as a simplified MARC method meant for more general description. MODS was designed to be more robust than Dublin Core, but less onerous than MARC. Each schema has detailed documentation about the fields and elements available online. Metadata creation often constitutes the most labor-intensive step in the digital collection publication process. Therefore, it may be desirable to provide only basic metadata for digital items.

Keep in mind robust metadata using the two schemas above ensures digital collections can be shared across platforms and institutions and items can be easily discovered and searched by patrons. When considering how to scale back metadata creation, consider the time and resources available to create metadata and to produce the most complete metadata possible during the time frame—favoring fields such as title, creator, subject, and description, which are needed for discovery and searching. Attending free or low-cost courses on metadata creation can also be enriching, especially because it can give library staff an opportunity to mingle with peers with experience creating and updating existing metadata for digital collections.

Summary of Common Digital Library Metadata Schemas

VRA Core
www.vraweb.org/projects/vracore4
This metadata schema is maintained by the Visual Resources Association and was designed specifically for description of works of visual culture as well as the surrogate images that document them.

Dublin Core
http://dublincore.org
The DC Initiative provides core metadata vocabularies with an emphasis on interoperability between systems. Although DC is often thought of as a description schema for digital collections, it was designed for general use. The DC schema contains fifteen elements.

MODS
www.loc.gov/standards/mods
MODS is a schema for a bibliographic element set designed specifically for use with library applications. It is maintained by the Library of Congress.

DIGITAL PRESERVATION

What should be done with preservation files once they are produced? There are several preservation concepts that are important for digital collection owners to understand—media storage, media dispersion, and media conversion. Where you choose to store digital files you create is of foremost importance. Large institutions have departments with systems experts who host servers and create plans for long-term digital storage. Small and one-person libraries might find professional photographers a closer model for preservation techniques. Many photographers use a series of external hard drives to store and backup digital files. Hard drives tend to have a lower failure rate than CDs and a lower rate of deterioration over time. If possible, it is a good idea to store backup hard drives as far away from active drives as possible. Large institutions accomplish this by dispersing materials geographically. Small and one-person libraries might be able to identify peer institutions—even those within the same city—that would be willing to swap storage space. At the very least, storing the files in two different rooms within the library is an attainable goal. Doing so is one way of safeguarding against environmental destruction including natural disasters. Finally, digital file conversion is an ongoing commitment. The 600 DPI TIFF files that are adequate for preservation today may be obsolete next year. Experts now think no one file format will remain infinitely active and that recurrent batch conversion of files will be standard practice for ensuring digital files can be read for years to come.

This discussion has so far considered only the digital files themselves. What about the metadata associated with each file? Considering the time spent creating metadata for each item, the metadata is almost more valuable than the digital file itself. Large institutions often use wrappers to envelop both the digital file and sophisticated descriptive and technical metadata—often in the form of METS—into one larger file containing all of the information needed to recreate the access display of that image. This is a highly technical process that might not be feasible for small and one-person libraries. Instead, think critically about how to preserve the metadata created for each item and associate it with the digital file. One simple method is to keep a spreadsheet that contains metadata associated with a collection of items in the same folder as the items themselves. The metadata is related to each item by a unique file name that should never be changed once metadata has been created. Whatever method you devise, ensure that a relationship readable by humans is established between the file and the metadata.

DIGITAL ASSESSMENT AND COLLECTION PROMOTION

If you have taken time to carefully digitize and describe worthwhile materials, you will want to see those materials used by patrons. The first step is to conduct analytics on your collection. If the content delivery system selected does not come with a built-in analytics feature, Google Analytics is a free option that is robust and easy to install. Any basic analytics system will collect data such as which items are most heavily used, which collections are most heavily used, how often your collection has visitors, and how long the average visitor viewed your materials. If these numbers are favorable, they can inform decisions about whether to continue or grow digitization projects.

Aside from making the collection easily available from your library web page, how can you drive online patrons to your new materials? One of the easiest low cost ways to promote collections is by using social media. This is especially effective if you begin a social media campaign in the early stages of the digitization project. Let patrons and stakeholders know what new collections they can look forward to in the future. As you digitize items, offer a sneak peek at them. When metadata is created, pass along interesting tidbits. When a collection is published, highlight jewels from the collection or spotlight items periodically.

Building a viable social media presence for digital collections can be demanding. By nature, social media outlets entail constant updates. If your digitization team includes several people, collaboratively promoting the collections via social media can distribute some of the burden. If you are working independently, creating a calendar for yourself with time allotted each day can help. For more information on developing library social media and social networking presences see chapter 8.

With analytics installed on digital collections, it is possible to monitor not only usage rates of collections, but also effectiveness of promotional efforts. The thing to remember about digital collection promotion is to be enthusiastic. Digital collections often represent some of the most exciting and unique materials libraries have to offer. Be creative about how to share these materials with patrons.

CONCLUSION

Hopefully, this chapter has demystified the digital collection creation process and demonstrated that digital projects can be feasible for small and one-person libraries. Once the technology, standards, and practices are generally understood, digital projects are no different from other projects. They require initial and continued planning and resources, but they can also be some of the most rewarding projects to initiate and execute.

Finding Help and Keeping Up with Changing Technology in Libraries

Rene J. Erlandson

Working in small or one-person libraries can be challenging, especially when problems and questions arise and there is no one within the library to go to for assistance. Therefore, establishing a network to obtain technology-related advice and help, beyond equipment warranty and software vendor customer assistance, is important.

Begin creating a support network by considering institutional relationships. If the library is part of a larger entity such as a local government or college or has a direct relationship to a larger entity, get to know the individuals responsible for technology issues and draw on their expertise. Most public and academic libraries are members of state and regional library agencies, consortia, or associations. Many of these organizations offer training and support through in-person or online workshops and conferences. Is the library part of a consortia or interest group whose membership could be tapped for advice? There are several user groups formed around library vendors such as Ex Libris Users of North America (ELUNA), Innovative Users Group (IUG) associated with Innovative Interfaces Inc. products, Customers of SirsiDynix Users Group Inc. (COSUGI), and a variety of OCLC user groups, to name just a few. User groups are a good way to obtain immediate help or advice via online electronic discussion lists and wikis from a network of individuals who use similar vendors or products. In addition, user groups often have national and regional conferences or meetings where librarians and vendor representatives offer workshops and training sessions.

When developing a technology-related support network, also consider libraries in the area that use the same integrated library system, interlibrary loan system, or bibliographic utility vendor or that have a similar technology configuration whose staff could be a resource. Build relationships with libraries that have a similar technology configuration whose staff could be resources. Most librarians are willing to share their technology expertise with colleagues or suggest others who might help. Also, consider partnering with other area libraries on new initiatives as a way to enhance expertise, share associated costs, and build broader support for the library.

A valuable free online resource for library staff is WebJunction (www.webjunction .org). Launched in 2003, the nonprofit site connects library staff across the country and hosts a variety of online forums and e-mail lists, including a technology forum and the Web4Lib electronic discussion list. The site also offers a variety of training resources and webinars that include technology topics.

If training on specific software packages is needed, consider subscribing to a cloud-based training service. Lynda.com is a low-cost ($25/month–$375/year) online training alternative that provides detailed, incremental training along with example exercises and files for software packages such as Adobe and Microsoft Office; for scripting languages such as HTML, Java, and JQuery; and for online services such as YouTube and Google Analytics. The service offers more than 700 online tutorials.

KEEPING UP WITH TRENDS AND EMERGING TECHNOLOGY

As discussed in previous chapters, maintaining technology initiatives is critical to long-term success. However, it is also important to keep up with the ebb and flow of technology trends and emerging technologies in order to plan for the future and efficiently deploy resources over time. Experience has shown that national technology trends quickly find their way into libraries. Therefore, it is essential to monitor technology developments outside of library science as well as within the field to anticipate future technology use in and impact on library services.

Industry

One way to keep an eye on technology industry trends is to set up an RSS feed reader or aggregator that will collate posts from a variety of popular national

Free Windows RSS Feed Readers/Aggregators

FeedDemon
www.feeddemon.com

Google Reader
www.google.com/reader

Feedreader
www.feedreader.com

Free iOS RSS Feed Readers/Aggregators

Shrook
www.utsire.com/shrook

Reeder
http://readerapp.com

Pulse
www.pulse.me

technology blogs and news sources into one location. Wired (www.wired.com) covers all things technology related and offers a number of tech-focused blogs to subscribe to as well as a general Top Stories option. Probably best known for its coverage of social media trends, Mashable (http://mashable.com) also offers readers news on digital culture and general technology issues and produces a number of blogs on these topics. While not as prolific as some blogs, ReadWriteWeb's (www .readwriteweb.com) Top Story offers a variety of daily news from the technol-ogy world. It is also useful to watch The Official Google Blog (http://googleblog .blogspot.com) and Apple Hot News (www.apple.com/hotnews) to find out what new products or services are in development or being launched from these industry leaders. comScore Voices (http://blog.comscore.com) is one of the best blogs for tracking trends in digital use, showing which services and developers are gain-ing (or losing) market share which translates into what services and products the public is using.

Library Science

A few options for keeping abreast of technology deployment and usage in librar-ies are blogs, discussion boards, and conferences. Participating in blogs and discussion boards is a simple and efficient way to keep up, as subscriptions and memberships are free and the only investment is the time required to set up an RSS reader, subscribe to feeds and discussion boards, and monitor them. While more costly to attend, technology-related sessions at professional conferences are useful for learning detailed information about deploying specific initiatives locally and discovering nuances of emerging technology that might be capitalized on by librarians in the future.

Popular Technology Blogs and News Sites

Wired
www.wired.com

Mashable
http://mashable.com

ReadWriteWeb's
www.readwriteweb.com

The Official Google Blog
http://googleblog.blogspot.com

Apple Hot News
www.apple.com/hotnews

comScore Voices
http://blog.comscore.com

ALA TechSource Blog
www.alatechsource.org/blog

Perpetual Beta
http://americanlibrariesmagazine
.org/perpetualbeta

iLibrarian
http://oedb.org/blogs/ilibrarian

NewsBreak/Weekly News Digest
www.infotoday.com

Blogs

Like the national technology news landscape, there are many technology-related blogs written by and for librarians. For general library technology news, subscribe to any of the blogs listed in the sidebar titled Popular Technology Blogs and News Sites. Blogs for specific aspects of technology in libraries such as e-books and e-resource management, library vendor blogs, and specific product blogs can be found through a simple keyword search via your search engine of choice.

Discussion Boards

Discussions of uses for emerging technologies in libraries and technology trends often show up on electronic discussion boards (also known as listservs) and blogs long before the same topics are addressed in conference workshops or sessions. Therefore, discussion boards are often the best way to stay current with technology-related topics in libraries.

Most online discussion boards have a setup option to receive posts individually as they are made or in digest form with all posts collated into one e-mail a day at the time of subscription. Some discussion boards are very active, with members passionately discussing a range of issues within the discussion board topic, while other boards have significantly fewer posts per day. Due to the amount of traffic on some lists, you may want to create a separate e-mail account to subscribe to the online boards.

To follow and participate in discussions of the broad topic of technology in libraries subscribe to one or both of the following lists: lita-1, the electronic discussion board for the Library and Information Technology Association (LITA) of ALA; or diglib-1, Digital Libraries Research mailing list of the International Federation of Library Associations (IFLA). There are also many online boards where discussions focus on narrow topics within library technology, such as:

Library Technology Discussion Boards

- lita-1
- diglib-1
- code4lib
- digipres

- acr-igdc-1
- alcts-eres
- ngc4lib
- Web4Lib

code4lib, a forum for library computer programming; digipres, a list for discussion of digital preservation issues; acr-igdc-1, where digital curation issues are discussed; alcts-eres, for discussion of electronic resource collection, management, and preservation; ngc4lib, focused on next generation catalogs in libraries; and Web4Lib, a forum for issues related to creating and managing library web servers, services, and applications. This is just a sampling of the library technology-related electronic discussion boards available.

129

Conferences

Participating in training and session opportunities at conferences is a great way to find out about technology trends in librarianship and learn how to implement specific initiatives locally. For American Library Association (ALA) Annual and Midwinter Conference attendees, LITA (Library and Information Technology Association) and ALA often sponsor tech trend sessions which are open to all conference attendees. National conferences focused solely on library technology-related topics, issues, and trends include Internet Librarian (www.infotoday.com/il2013); Code{4}

Library Technology Conferences

Internet Librarian
www.infotoday.com/il2013

Code{4}lib
http://code4lib.org/conference

LITA National Forum
www.ala.org/ala/lita/
conferences

Library Technology Conference
http://libtechconf.org

Brick and Click
http://brickandclick.org

lib (http://code4lib.org/conference); and LITA National Forum (www.ala.org/lita/conferences). Also look for technology-related sessions at local or statewide library association conferences or meetings. Regional library technology conferences like Library Technology Conference (http://libtechconf.org) in Minnesota and Brick and Click (http://brickandclick.org) symposium in Missouri attract high-quality speakers from across the nation and are more economical to attend than national conferences.

CONCLUSION

Individuals working in small and one-person libraries generally have multiple roles and face diverse demands at any given time; therefore, it is important to build a support network you can count on for assistance and find simple methods for keeping up with what is happening on the library technology landscape.

Glossary

access file. Surrogate derived from the preservation file that has been edited and sized for online display.

aggregator. Independent electronic resources gathered under an umbrella by vendors and offered to subscribers/purchases.

analytics. Automated data collection about traffic and usage trends of an online resource such as a digital collection or digital item.

authorized users. In relation to a license agreement, categories of individuals and their affiliation to the library who are permitted to use licensed resources (i.e., faculty, staff, students, walk-in users, etc.).

blog. Publicly accessible interactive website (or weblog) frequently updated by a specific individual or group of individuals with news, opinions, events, videos, images, etc.

breach remedy/cure. Section of electronic resource license that states how licensor will communicate breach of license and how much time will be allotted for licensee to cure the breach before access is suspended.

click-through license agreement. Contractual agreement a user views online and accepts terms of, by clicking on a box or button indicating the user's assent.

client-server network. Network architecture in which powerful computers (servers) manage resources, applications, and traffic for less powerful computers (clients).

cloud computing. Service by which resources, software, and information are delivered over the Internet on demand.

content delivery system. A comprehensive tool for upload, manipulation, and display of digital items and related metadata.

content management system (CMS). Collection of procedures used to collaboratively manage website content.

Creative Commons. License agreements that allow content creators to communicate the rights they reserve and waive for the benefit of users and other creators.

digital SLR (digital single-lens reflex). A digital camera that uses a mechanical mirror system to direct light through the lens to the image sensor.

dots per inch (DPI). A print term that describes the number of dots per square inch of halftone print; now used interchangeably with PPI, or pixels per inch, to describe the same phenomenon as displayed on electronic screens.

Dublin Core. Metadata schema designed for describing general items in digital collections.

encryption. Code used to prevent unauthorized access to or eavesdropping of data transmissions.

enterprise software. Software used by businesses or government agencies as part of a computer-based information system such as human resource management, resource planning, security, content management, and automated billing and payment processing.

firewall. Security software used to block unauthorized incoming and outgoing network traffic.

force majeure. Neither licensor nor licensee will be liable for any damages or have the right to terminate the agreement if caused by circumstances beyond its control such as acts of nature, government restrictions, wars, etc.

governing law. In a license agreement, the jurisdiction under which a license will be interpreted according to the laws of that particular country, state, county, or province.

grant of license. Section of license agreement that officially states the licensor grants the licensee nonexclusive access of the resource.

Gretag Macbeth ColorChecker. Commonly used target for color management of digital files.

hardware life cycle. Elapsed amount of time between purchase and replacement of technology hardware.

hypertext markup language (HTML). Markup symbols or code included in files for display on the World Wide Web.

Internet protocol address (IP address). 32-bit or 128-bit numerical label assigned to each device communicating within a computer network using Internet protocol.

Indemnity. In an electronic resource license, the statement or section that exempts licensor and/or licensee from liability for claims against, losses or damages.

interlibrary loan. Library lending and borrowing to and from other libraries.

joint photographic experts group (JPEG). The most commonly used lossy compressed file format for access files; file extension is .jpg.

JPEG 2000. The most recently released, though not yet widely adopted, version of JPEG.

license agreement. A legal contract between two parties, the licensor and the licensee.

local area network (LAN). A network constrained by a limited physical area, like a single building.

machine-readable cataloging (MARC). Data format and set of standards commonly used by libraries to describe book materials.

media access control address (MAC address). Registered identification number, most often assigned by the manufacturer of a network interface card (NIC). Also known as an Ethernet hardware address (EHA) or a physical address.

metadata. Data that describe one or more aspects of other data; content about content; information that describes and adds context to the digital items included in collections; often divided into descriptive, administrative, and structural metadata.

Metadata Encoding and Transmission Standard (METS). Metadata standard for encoding descriptive, administrative, and structural metadata into XML.

Metadata Object Description Schema (MODS). A metadata schema designed for describing general items in digital collections to a greater degree than Dublin Core, but a lesser degree than MARC.

network drop cable. Cable that runs from the local hub to the office wall box; can have more than one network jack (IP address/box).

networking. The connecting together of computers to share files and resources.

open-source software (OSS). Free application software and associated source code available to the general public for use and modification.

passive agreement. Electronic resources license that requires only one signature, often the licensee's, or none at all.

peer-to-peer (P2P) network. Distributed network architecture in which computers within the network are equally privileged and share tasks, loads, and resources directly without a central server.

perpetual access. When the library has attained the right to ongoing access for electronic resources either after the subscription has expired or if purchased as a one-time shot.

preservation files. Uncompressed, unprocessed digital files that are captured in a way that entails the least amount of processing as possible; often include borders and targets such as a WhiBal card or Gretag Macbeth ColorChecker; captured and preserved at the highest practical resolution.

proprietary software. Computer programs exclusively owned by a specific company or individual that may be used by a purchaser or licensee under certain conditions but that may not be copied, distributed, or modified by purchaser or licensee.

QR code (Quick Response code). Mobile device readable barcode linked to information, websites, images, etc.

really simple syndication (RSS). Standard used by publishers to automatically syndicate frequently updated web content.

RFP (request for proposal). A request for proposal (RFP) is a formal document asking for bids for a product and service.

rootkit. A set of software tools that enables unidentified, unauthorized administrator-level access to a restricted (or privileged) computer by subverting standard operating system functionality.

screencasting. Digitally recorded computer screen output and audio input shared with others in video format, also known as screen capture.

Shared Electronic Resource Understanding (SERU). Developed by the National Information Standards Organization (NISO), an agreement by which vendors/publishers and electronic resource subscribers agree to operate within a framework of shared understanding and good faith.

signal-to-noise ratio. The digital equivalent of graininess in traditional photography; a comparison of the desired signal to the level of background noise.

site definition. The section of a license that specifies covered physical locations where licensed resource may be used.

sniffing. Sniffing, or packet sniffing, is the practice of intercepting network traffic with the intent of analyzing or interpreting patterns in the traffic, or gathering information passed through the network. Sniffing can be used for good things, like monitoring network traffic patterns, or bad things, like stealing passwords.

social media. User-generated online content such as blogs, wikis, videos, photos, tagging, etc., (content centric).

social networking. Online websites that facilitate communication among members. The sites allow members to make and manage connections and relationships.

spyware. Independent executable programs used to gather personal information about Internet users such as credit card numbers, e-mail addresses, passwords, and web surfing habits by unauthorized monitoring of keystrokes.

tagged image file format (TIFF). The most commonly used uncompressed file format for images; file extension is .tif.

technology plan. Document containing overview of past, present, and future technology goals and objectives used to guide organizational technology decision making.

Trojan horse. A nonreplicating malicious program that masquerades as a benign application but that can ultimately delete files, transmit sensitive data such as passwords, and provide complete unauthorized access to a system.

Visual Resources Association core (VRA core). Metadata schema designed for describing images in digital collections.

WAMP. Web development platform used to create programs that use the Microsoft Windows operating system; Apache web server; MySQL database; and PHP, Perl, or Python scripting languages.

web analytics. Data collection, measurement, and report generation of traffic to and within a website.

web page. Document or location on the World Wide Web that is accessible via a web browser.

website. Multiple web pages linked together by developer.

WhiBal. Commonly used target for color management of digital files.

wide area network (WAN). Computer networks that cover multiple geographic areas, such as multiple buildings or towns.

Wi-Fi (wireless-fidelity). A wireless local area network that uses radio waves to pass information between electronic devices such as computers, printers, scanners, etc.

wiki. Website collaboratively developed and edited by a community of users via a web browser.

wired networking. Use of Ethernet cabling, servers, hubs, switches, and file sharing to connect computers.

wireless access point (WAP). A device that acts as a central transmitter and receiver for a wireless network. Wireless access points often act as a connector between a wired network and a wireless network.

worm. A self-replicating malicious computer program that gains unauthorized access to a computer network via one machine and sends copies of itself to other computers on the network minimally causing increased bandwidth consumption.

About the Authors and Contributors

AUTHORS

Rene J. Erlandson

Rene J. Erlandson is the director of virtual services at the University of Nebraska Omaha (UNO) libraries, with oversight of computer systems, digital asset management, digital collection development, electronic resource management, emerging technologies, library systems, network infrastructure, and Web development. Prior to joining the University of Nebraska faculty, she worked at University of Illinois Urbana-Champaign (UIUC) and Iowa State University for two decades. As the senior cataloger and project coordinator for the Library of Congress-administered Illinois Newspaper Project at UIUC, she visited many small libraries throughout the state of Illinois and was often consulted on technology questions by librarians working in those libraries.

Rachel A. Erb

Rachel A. Erb has been working in technical services for over a decade with substantial experience in cataloging materials of various formats and in managing integrated library systems. She recently transitioned to focusing on electronic resources and is now the electronic resources management librarian at Colorado State University (CSU). She is familiar with the challenges solo practitioners face because most of her professional experience consists of working in either rural settings with limited resources or regional state universities. She has also written several case studies of technical services operations in these environments.

CONTRIBUTORS

SCOTT CHILDERS is the emerging technologies librarian at the University of Nebraska–Lincoln (UNL). He earned his BS in computer science at UNL and his MLS from Emporia State University. Scott has written and presented on technology topics affecting the library field for over a decade and is a former president of the Nebraska Library Association.

R. NICCOLE WESTBROOK has nearly a decade of experience building digital collections for a variety of institutions and audiences. She currently works as the coordinator of digital operations at the University of Houston Libraries where she is responsible for the UH Digital Library and the UH Digital Library Internship Program—both of which she helped to grow from concept to final product. Her current research focuses on efficient digital library workflows and online management techniques.

MARTA DEYRUP is the Neal-Schuman development editor for this project.

Index